Your Pets
Past Lives

& How They Can Heal You

Your Pets' Past Lives

& How They Can Heal You

Madeleine Walker

FINDHORN PRESS

Published in 2012 by Findhorn Press, Scotland.

ISBN 978-1-84409-572-8

Quotes:
Quote on p. 125 is from *Your Soul's Plan: Discovering the Real Meaning of the Life
You Planned Before You Were Born* by Robert Schwartz, published by Frog Books/
North Atlantic Books, copyright © 2009 by Robert Schwartz.
Reprinted by permission of publisher.

Photography:
Flick Cromak p. 131, Sylvia Davalos p. 69, Fiona Habershon p. 84,
Sera Henbest p. 90, Leigh Jackson p. 13, Pam Lovett p. 31/34,
Victoria Standen p. 58, Cynthia Starkey p. 105.

Edited by Jacqui Lewis
Cover and Interior design by Damian Keenan
Printed and bound in the EU

1 2 3 4 5 6 7 8 9 17 16 15 14 13 12

Published by
Findhorn Press
117-121 High Street,
Forres IV36 1AB,
Scotland, UK

t +44 (0)1309 690582
f +44 (0)131 777 2711
e info@findhornpress.com
www.findhornpress.com

dedication

*To my father David, my brother Andrew
and all my family, both human and animal,
who enrich my life in so many ways.*

Contents

A human heart once expanded by love,
never again regains its original dimensions.
ANONYMOUS

Foreword

by Jenny Smedley, best-selling author of
Pets Have Souls Too and *Pets Are Forever*

I believe that an understanding of who we really are, and an acceptance that our souls have evolved through many lifetimes, is vital both to our survival as humans and to the progress of our spirit into something much more wonderful than we can even imagine. I also believe that animals are our spiritual teachers. If we are to survive on this planet we're allowed and privileged to call home, then we need to understand and accept that animals are a part of us, and that our fates are inextricably intertwined. Those who harm either the bodies or the spirits of animals do immeasurable harm to the entire ecosystem of both the earth and all of those that live there.

Madeleine Walker's new book brings both my most cherished concepts together in one place. She demonstrates compellingly not only that animals are our spiritual teachers, and that their welfare is paramount for ours, but also that they can heal the past for us. Her journeys and insights show that animals are closer to us in spirit than even the most ardent animal lover could have realized. That we have certain pets that we feel inextricably attached to is a natural phenomenon, because these animals are literally a spark of our souls. They have travelled with us through lifetimes and often go through great hardship in order to help our soul's progress and be with us through our human trials and tribulations.

Going even further than that, Madeleine has developed a new and unique way of enabling animals, both domesticated and wild, to help us unravel and re-record aspects of past lives that are holding us back in this lifetime. She is one of the rarest people in the world, in that she has developed a system for connecting with wild animals and learning lessons from them about the planet and about ourselves, which will empower us, if like her, we develop the ability to listen and to hear. She has also developed a way to access our pets' spirits and enable a connection with them to help us to 'rewrite the script' of our past, thereby changing our future. We're very lucky that Madeleine is so willing to share her abilities with us in this book.

My advice is to turn the pages of this book with an open mind and an open heart. Embrace the possibilities within and I believe you'll be able to open a whole new, exciting and fulfilling chapter of your life. This book will enrich the reader. If you're already an animal lover and believe in their soul connection to us, this book will enrapture you and bring you huge enjoyment. If you need convincing that animals are more than just slaves put here for the gratification and amusement of humans, then it's absolutely vital for you to read this book. Man must wake up to the messages the animals are sending us.

It came to me that every time I lose a dog
they take a piece of my heart with them.
And every new dog who comes into my life,
gifts me with a piece of their heart.
If I live long enough,
all the components of my heart will be dog,
And I will become as generous and loving
as they are.

AUTHOR UNKNOWN

Introduction

Have you ever thought that the only 'person' who truly understands you or knows exactly where you're coming from is your pet? I had a miserable time at school, and I would come home and just cuddle my old corgi Rufus. He instinctively knew just what to do to cheer me up; as I sought solace in his company, he'd either play the court jester, or just let me sob into his fur. He'd gaze deep into my eyes with such a knowing look, as though he understood exactly what I was feeling. So many people say to me that they feel their pet is their soulmate and that they have better relationships and feelings of unconditional love with them than with any human counterpart. Why is this? Why can we love our animals unreservedly and feel that love reciprocated on such deep levels? Why are they so important to us? A few years ago I became interested in past-life trauma and how it might affect our present lives. I discovered issues buried deep within me that were explained by delving into my past. I also discovered that I could reclaim healing tools that I had used in previous lifetimes as a healer and shaman. I believe that our past shapes who we are today. Little did I realize then the deep significance of my discoveries, and how they would lead me into new territory as a therapist and how my new animal clients would educate me in the deeper concepts of past-life connections.

Much has been written about the human soul and that we may travel in soul 'groups', often meeting up again in another life, in another guise. Through my work as a horse-and-rider trauma consultant, animal intuitive, empowerment coach and emotional healer, I have been made aware of a much deeper concept. The animals have taught me that they too travel with us and because we have become so 'westernized' and materialistic, and distanced from our inner selves, they can be better equipped to tune in to what may be necessary to heal us on a soul level. I suppose I have been called an animal whisperer, but I believe the animals help me to go far deeper than that. I have been guided by the animals to connect with the soul essence of people and animals and, in fact, in my travels, wild creatures like the cetaceans (whales) have helped me connect to the soul of the planet. Connecting and communicating with the animals flags up issues that need to be addressed, in both themselves and in their owners. I come across countless cases where animals are desperate to help, and through subsequent sessions with the owners, numerous issues are dealt with and cleared.

This book describes how animals can commit to reincarnating to help with their owners' unresolved issues, or to continue supporting them on their soul journeys.

When working with animals in the wild, too, I am amazed at their messages of wisdom for mankind and the planet. This book contains many case studies, drawn from clients who have been able to address self-limiting and destructive issues and release chronic physical challenges with help from their animal companions. These amazing cases are of animals that are so in tune with their owners that they can flag up present and past-life traumas. These challenges are impactful and debilitating and often prevent the person from reaching their true potential and fulfilment.

Animals also give us the gift of emotional release through tears. In human relationships or emotions, we are often not able to cry; we can sometimes bury our emotions very deep within us, which can result in physical conditions and deteriorating health. Our animals somehow manage to help us access those emotions; so, although we may think that we are releasing and expressing emotions connected to the animal, we may in fact be expressing and relieving the emotional tension that we store within us from many differing causes.

So what gifts we are given by our animal friends, who commit to helping us again and again! Some of the concepts in this book may seem a little far-fetched — they did to me when I was first made aware of them. I feel as though I have been taken on a roller coaster of emotions and zoomed up through a vertical learning curve. The animals have taken me on a journey of discovery and teaching, supporting me along the way, bringing in new techniques when I was ready to accept them. For example, horses have shown me techniques such as soul retrieval, which is a shamanic technique performed by ancient indigenous healers; a damaged part of a person, detached due to trauma, can be reclaimed and a person can be made whole again. The animals have taught me that this can happen with them too, in either past or current incarnations.

The animals have also taught me how to remove negative energy and entities that may be creating physical and emotional limitations. I have discovered so much about myself, and am so humbled by the wisdom of the animals and their ability to heal us. I am driven by them to get their message of love out there and to raise awareness of the power of their message, not only for us but also for our beautiful planet.

Sam the Puppy

The first animal that ever 'talked' to me was a Jack Russell puppy called Sam. Not only did I hear him talking very clearly in my head, which was weird enough, the subject matter also blew my mind. He 'told' me that he was a reincarnation of his owner's old dog and that he had returned to continue supporting her through the difficult life she had chosen. He then showed me what he had looked like in his past incarnation. At this stage I was ready to call in the men in the white coats, but when I checked with his owner, she verified everything that the puppy had told me and even showed me a photograph of her old dog, which looked exactly as the puppy had shown me.

As I began to understand more and more about the role of the animals, the right cases found me to help me to deepen my knowledge. The animals have guided me every step of the way, helping me work through the sometimes chronic emotional and physical issues that arise in both pets and their owners.

As I learn more and more, I am constantly amazed at the ability the animals have to help us move forwards in our lives. Little did I realize, when I used to cuddle Rufus, just how much animals would feature in my adult life, turning it upside down with strange new concepts that they have helped me assimilate and use for the benefit of others. Sometimes when I am shown a past-life trauma by an animal, I wonder how on earth I am going to explain or describe the scenario — they can be quite shocking. Somehow, though, the animals help me to find the right words that gently coax their human companion towards awareness. The person, although at times initially sceptical, will suddenly feel something resonating deep within them and begin to feel emotions or increased physical symptoms. The animals then guide us through a process of release and a regaining of empowerment. I believe the following chapters will help to broaden and empower you and encourage you to look at your animal friends in a very different way, appreciating just how amazing they are and also just how special you must be for them to have chosen to work with you. We are all amazing sentient beings on a journey; thank goodness we have so much help along the way!

CHAPTER 1

Why do our pets' past lives affect us?

Ireceive many requests for readings from people who are struggling with their connections to their pets or are overwhelmed by guilt or grief. I always feel this is very positive, as our pets allow us to access emotions that we may have learned to bury. We can be very expert at this, screwing down a nice tight lid on things and determined to 'soldier on'; but unfortunately bottling things up like this can lead to physical symptoms as our bodies try to process the emotions held deep within us. Pioneers in this concept — wonderful people like Louise Hay and Brandon Bays — generally refer to, and help people access, issues in their current life. But what is different and amazing about our pets is that they can help us access issues that stem from a root cause much farther back — from our past lives. When we can delve into the past like this, much can be explained, as these past circumstances and events can colour how we feel about ourselves in our current lives, as well as shaping and moulding our belief systems. When an animal shows us why we feel the way we do about ourselves or certain events and triggers in our lives, it can make sense of something — a phobia or a fear, for example — that we might not previously have been able to understand.

Rosanna, Gaia and Fantasia — Message from Atlantis

I did the following reading for an Italian lady, Rosanna, who was feeling very guilty about a cat called Gaia. She had rescued the cat, but had felt unable to keep her as she was inundated with other animals and was wearing herself out emotionally, physically and financially. The other cats already living in her home had not taken kindly to having yet another occupant and had refused to let Gaia into the house, so she was living in the barn while Rosanna tried, without success, to get the others to accept her. It was lovely to connect with Gaia to hear her side of things, in order to help this wonderful woman who tried so hard to home so many animals in need.

Gaia does seem to have an energy of abandonment about her, which is probably why she needs the reassurance of a home so much. I think the situation where she has become a little detached from you is probably good, in that she should be able to settle at her new home better now, so don't blame or upset yourself. You do have to think of your other cats first. I think the gift of Gaia coming to you is huge, and does relate to past-life issues with you and your animal friends. I feel that she has brought up a lot of feelings of guilt within you and that you have been punishing yourself because of the situation with her, when after all you have only done your best to help her in the best way you can under the circumstances.

It would be so much better for her to have a forever loving home that can cope with her condition. I feel you really push yourself and are very self-critical. I feel that in a past life you felt you let others down—animals and people—and it seems that this lifetime is all about you resolving this by helping animals so much. It feels, though, that sometimes you give too much of yourself and don't always look after YOU! You are really important because if anything happened to you, the animals would be in trouble! You are such an earth angel and Gaia's arrival is the catalyst for this to come to the surface. We are not meant to all live together for ever; sometimes there are other solutions—just as with human relationships, with animals sometimes there has to be a parting in order for each individual to go forwards on their soul journey. You have given so much love to Gaia and given her a home and now you both know on a deep level that there was a time limit on that connection, which as I say, is nonetheless very important to have made. I have had to rehome animals myself in the past, which has really upset me, but I have known that it was the right thing to do by them—it helps to ask yourself "What is the best outcome for them?" You have nothing to reproach yourself for. Gaia has learned from you as well. It has been just as important for her to realize that she is loved and cared for and that she is worthy of that love and care, which she will get in even greater amounts in her new home.

I feel you were a horse dealer in a past life and that you were not always very scrupulous as to where the horses went as long as you made money from them. I think sometimes you promised owners that you would find very caring homes but in the end you didn't care, you just sold them for the highest price. I think there is one horse with you now—a horse that's very special to you—which was with you in that lifetime. I think it was the one horse that touched your heart in that past life and it came to a very bad end, which finally made you realize how materialistic and uncaring of animals' feelings you had been. Of course it had been sent to you to teach you that, as your animals and Gaia have been sent to you once again in this life. Your agreement for this present incarnation is to always do your best by the animals, but to also honour yourself. Sometimes we have to experience both sides of the coin in order to learn the most! I have had a past life where I was not kind to animals, and that is why I am so committed to doing my best to heal them and their human carers in this lifetime! Animals are amazing because they are willing to teach us so much through their own hardships. So thank Gaia for all that she has taught you, listen to her words and know, without doubt, that you are doing a great job. She will be fine at her new home. There is a Bach flower remedy, Walnut, that could help her settle; it will also be very good for any of your animals who are traumatized by their rescue and are unsettled. Perhaps you could mention this to your friend who is willing to take Gaia, if she seems a little worried in her new home? You can order these remedies online—or you may already use them?

The Australian bush flower remedy Bush Fuchsia could be very useful for you. It brings about a real sense of balance and inner calm. I feel this will help you to feel a lot better about yourself and your situations, so maybe you could see whether it feels right for you.

I do hope this helps. Let me know if you are confused or unsure of anything, and I will try and explain better. But in short, Gaia will be fine—and remember to look after your own well-being too!

After reading this, Rosanna told me about the horse, Fantasia, that she felt Gaia was referring to and asked me to make a connection between them as well.

Healing, Forgiveness, Acceptance and Release

These are the key words that underpin your connections with all the animals and yourself. I typed 'Healing' and 'Release' and now Gaia keeps asking me to add more words—first 'Forgiveness' and now 'Acceptance'.

This is all about Atlantis and it was the past-life trauma that I was referring to in your reading before. This was the time when I was unkind to animals. Fantasia is one of the few Atlantean 'golden' horses. They are always chestnut, and generally have a special whorl of hair somewhere on their body, usually on their head. She is such a wise ancient being and it's obvious now why she came up in Gaia's reading. Remember she talked about the special horse in your life? Your connection with her is very important and she will teach you so much about yourself. She says you still don't accept or forgive yourself on this very deep soul level. Like me, you have committed to working as hard as you can to help and heal as many animals as you can, but also like me, you may be forgetting to help and heal yourself. When I went swimming with wild dolphins in the Red Sea, they gave me some profound information about their connection to Atlantis and told me that many of us humans also have these connections. Although we do not realize it, we are carrying guilt from the downfall of Atlantis, which prevents us from truly forgiving ourselves on a deep soul level. The dolphins say that this clearing of the parasitic dark energies that still weave their roots within our DNA has to happen now, so we can be free from making the same mistakes from the past over again. I hope this doesn't sound too weird and I didn't mention Atlantis before because I wasn't sure how open you were to it. But having now met you, I know you will try to understand the very profound message and healing that Fantasia and all your animals are facilitating within your psyche. Fantasia was with you in Atlantis during its golden age, when everything was about love and healing. Initially the new genetic-engineering techniques were to be for the betterment of the different species—to cure any dis-ease. But greed took over and we got sucked into the feeling of power that this technical knowledge gave us. I wasn't directly involved in the mutations, but I did nothing to stop it when it went out of control. Fantasia says your intentions were honourable at first, but by the time you realized what suffering had ensued and the imminent downfall of the civilization, it was too late. I hope this doesn't sound too weird. Even as I'm typing this I'm feeling Fantasia's almost desperation to try to explain it to you. I have never given a reading quite like this before—it's like her hooves are typing this!

The other lifetime as the horse dealer had to happen so that Fantasia could once again come into your life and affect the way you treated and understood animals. I did a regression where I went back to that time, and I felt so terrible when I realized what I had been involved in. I think I need to go back and heal it, as I haven't done this yet and still feel as if I'm paying penance for it. Fantasia says you are too—she says everything you have been through on all levels is connected to the punishment you are still giving yourself. So thank you again, because I need to look at that too! It's like we can never feel fully healed or feel total love for ourselves until we finally resolve and release these things. I think many animal lovers who sacrifice so much of themselves for their animals, not looking after themselves, are trying to compensate for past trauma and guilt.

Sit quietly with Fantasia and 'tell' her that you understand why this has surfaced. Ask her to show you how to release it. I'm sure she will be happy to help you. You can either say this out loud or form the words in your head, sending out love from your heart. Perhaps you can imagine you both wrapped in the pink light of unconditional love and forgiveness as you ascend to the light from your deaths in that sad lifetime. See what comes to your mind.

Fantasia

What she is saying is that none of the past matters now—it's about how we respond to the planet and all its inhabitants now. These are very big concepts and you might feel that you are a tiny and insignificant part, but in your love for and development of your fantastic work, you are well on the way to raising awareness of the messages and needs of our beautiful spiritual horses.

Gaia and Fantasia are also talking about a black horse that has needed a lot of help, but has also taught you a lot. I think this horse challenged your previous beliefs about how horses should be ridden and treated. Again I know that Gaia was sent to you to bring up these feelings of guilt that we talked about before. She is not sure about her age but she's telling me her birth sign is Pisces, which I feel is also connected to the Atlantean ocean energies. I feel that she was previously with someone who just moved away and didn't bother to find a new home for her or consider her needs at all. I'm glad that you have worked through your problems with keeping her. Fantasia would prefer this reading to be on a much deeper scale—she gets frustrated when I stop to ask questions about age, etc., and says that these things are not important. What is important, she says, is to understand and act on the messages that she is sending you.

So see what happens when you sit with her, and let me know. Use the pink light and see how that makes you feel—and give me lots of feedback, so that I can help if needs be.

Sending lots of pink love to you and all your beautiful animals!

Let a horse whisper in your ear
and breathe on your heart ...
you will never regret it.
AUTHOR UNKNOWN

Chloe and Sue — Healing Pain

I was recently called out to a horse that felt responsible for its current owner's death in a previous life they had shared, and that had returned to heal that trauma and ensure the safety of its owner in this lifetime. The owner, Sue, asked me to call in to see her young horse, Chloe, as she felt that Chloe was grumpy and sometimes downright miserable. She had bought Chloe as a young foal and had always treated her well; in fact, Sue adored her. I questioned Sue about her feelings when she had first laid eyes on Chloe. Sue said that Chloe had strode straight up to her and nudged her as if to say 'Take me home'. The last thing Sue had intended was to buy such a young horse, but something in Chloe's expression compelled her to bring her home to her Devon farm.

As I quietly entered the stable, Chloe put her ears back and pulled a rather ugly face at me. In my head I heard her say, "She doesn't understand! I need to prove myself. I need to show her that I'm safe and that I love her!" Chloe was only two years old, too young to be ridden, but it seemed that Chloe's mood swings were due to the frustration she felt at not getting the chance to show that she was sensible and that she would protect Sue from harm. Poor Chloe showed me that terrible event from the past life she shared with Sue. She had been carrying Sue up a steep mountainside, had lost her footing and they had both fallen. Sue's back was broken and she was crushed beneath Chloe and, tragically, they both perished. Chloe told me that she felt entirely responsible for Sue's death, and the depth of her sorrow brought tears to my eyes. She then went on to tell me that Sue was still experiencing terrible problems with her back in this lifetime; then she gently nuzzled the base of Sue's spine to show me where the pain was. As I relayed this to Sue she started to cry as we all felt the depth of emotional despair that Chloe had been carrying. Sue couldn't believe that Chloe was able to tell me about her back pain and pinpoint the exact spot where her back had been operated on. Sue also said that Chloe always seemed a lot more agitated when the other horses in the yard were ridden, and Chloe told me that she just wanted to be with them and be 'grown up'. Quite apart from the feeling of being left behind, she was frustrated at not getting the opportunity to show what a safe horse she was.

Sue promised Chloe that she would lead or long-rein her out on the road so that she could show how sensible she was, but there was still the problem of her back pain. Suddenly Chloe bent down to place her muzzle on the base of Sue's back and, closing her eyes, appeared to take deep breaths that she then blew out, soft and warm, onto the painful spot. Chloe's eyes were half closed and I could see and feel her concentration as she focussed her breath on the site of Sue's pain. I asked Sue what she could feel, and she replied that her whole back felt warm, almost glowing, and as if sharp crystalline forms were melting. The pain vanished from Sue's back and I was guided to ask her to visualize riding Chloe bareback, galloping across a beautiful meadow. Chloe particularly wanted me to emphasize how surefooted she was and to ask Sue to notice how safe she felt. I visualized this scene and felt Chloe's relief. Her eyes seemed much softer and her whole expression far happier. She seemed happy that she had been able to tell her story and that Sue knew now why she had seemed so depressed. She was very happy at the prospect of being trusted to behave on the road and looked forward to the day when she could be backed and ridden. I left Sue giving Chloe the biggest hug. The feedback from her was that she had stopped taking painkillers, as since Chloe had performed the healing, she'd had no more pain in her back.

Phiff and Karen — Discovering Hidden Talents

On one of my visits to France, I was asked to talk to a lovely horse called Phiff. His owner Karen was having great difficulties with him, due to his separation anxiety when his fieldmate was taken out for a ride and Phiff was left at home. They had even bought a donkey as a companion for him, but nothing seemed to help. Phiff just whinnied inconsolably and charged around the field, in dire danger of seriously injuring himself as he galloped flat out downhill and hurled his body at the fence, barely skidding to a stop in time to avoid it. If he were put in a stable, he would try to jump out or wreck it. He wasn't safe enough to ride out as he was unpredictable, so Solo, a gentle, safe bay hack who had become Phiff's best friend, had been bought for Karen to have some fun on.

Unfortunately, the problem with Phiff was spoiling everyone's enjoyment of their relationship. Phiff had been given to Karen because his previous owner became unwell and was frightened of his erratic behaviour. Karen hoped that she would be able to calm him down and have a harmonious relationship with him, but so far this was not happening. Again, I was amazed at the Universe's orchestration in bringing everyone back together in order to heal the past.

I arrived at Karen's beautiful home and was greeted by an assortment of dogs and cats, who all ran out wagging and purring in great excitement. They all had something to say about what was going on, and I had to ask them to slow down and speak one at a time, as I was being telepathically deafened! They intimated that Karen had to sort this out now and that Phiff had been behaving as dramatically as he had so that the situation could finally be resolved. I told Karen this and she admitted that for the life of her she couldn't remember why she had agreed to take Phiff on, as his reputation was fairly tarnished. She had just said yes without really knowing why, which is a common occurrence when the Universe is at work! However all was to be revealed when I made my way into the field to meet Phiff, his bay friend Solo, and the lovable donkey, who had the biggest, fluffiest ears I think I'd ever seen.

Phiff immediately made me feel very anxious as I tuned into his energy field. He gave me a picture of a knight in armour and what I felt was Phiff in this incarnation, a big black charger. He showed me Solo as a heavier horse, but still bay, with another knight riding him. I felt that Karen had been Phiff's knight. The trauma they'd experienced was a kind of trap that was set in a castle; they had tried to escape and gallop to safety in the woods where Solo and his rider were waiting. Unfortunately they had somehow fallen into a moat and to their deaths as they had tried to leap from the battlements. Their lives had ended because Phiff couldn't get back to Solo, which explained some of his desperation in his current life. I asked Karen if she had any interest in medieval times, as sometimes we can be very drawn to a particular era or country if we have experienced a past life there. She said that she'd recently experienced a very strange event that she really couldn't explain.

Phiff and Karen

A month before she'd been asked to take part in a medieval pageant and jousting exhibition and, without really knowing why, she'd vol- unteered to have a go at the jousting. She amazed herself and her onlookers by handling the lance with consummate ease. She seemed to instinctively know what to do, wielding it effortlessly and with great expertise, much to everyone's astonishment—especially her own. Now she knew why it had been so easy—she'd had lots of practice in her previous life as a knight.

When I asked her to tune into this past life, although I didn't give her many details, she described exactly what she and Phiff had looked like and the feelings of despair and fear as she realized their fate at the treachery that had befallen them. I had just been shown the past-life script rewrite technique, so I suggested that she contrived to visualize a far happier outcome. Phiff had completely calmed down by this point and was standing breathing very deeply with his eyes shut, as though willing a better ending. Karen visualized them leaping to safety and escaping just in time, galloping away at top speed into the forest and meeting their friend who was waiting for them.

I also felt that Phiff and Solo may have been foals together earlier in that life, as they had such a deep connection in this lifetime. I asked Karen to totally embrace the feeling of relief at their safe escape and reunion. Karen had become quite emotional and Phiff started to give the most enormous yawns, releasing all the tension that had been stored in his body for so long. Karen also revealed that she had been feeling very disempowered, without really knowing why, and that trust had always been a difficult issue for her. She said that she was suddenly feeling much stronger and more confident in herself, and that certain challenges she was facing seemed much more achievable—in other words, she trusted in a far better outcome than she had originally feared. We also 'told' Phiff that when Solo left the field it would only ever be for a short while and they would never be separated again. Karen was even hopeful that Phiff would now be calm enough to be ridden; then she could find someone to ride Solo and they could go out together.

Karen seemed to have a new sense of confidence in her abilities, which I felt sure would rub off on Phiff. I was amazed to hear about the jousting and I marvelled at the thought that we never know what we're capable of until we give it a try—who knows, each one of us could have some wonderful latent talent that has laid beneath the surface of our psyche for hundreds of years! It's exciting what you can find out about yourself when you revisit a past life, as the next case also illustrates.

Raoul and Kate — Back to the Plains

Not all past lives are traumatic or need to be healed. I visited a very troubled horse called Raoul, a top-class dressage horse who had been brutally treated where he lived in Spain. He had been so conditioned into absolute obedience and subservience that he had no idea how to express himself or what his real identity was. He was completely robotic in his performance and was too scared to be anything else in case of dire consequences. He was kept stabled and, as a stallion, was rarely allowed any time outside; on the rare occasions that he was allowed outside, he was alone in a small dirt compound. He had no social skills as he was never allowed the freedom to mix with other horses. He was sold as he was deemed not good enough to compete for the top competitions. He had been gelded and was depressed and painfully thin when he was rescued and brought to England to live with his wonderful present owner, Kate. As she was only just learning to work with natural horsemanship and just wanted a happy hack, it made no logical sense to buy a very high-class dressage horse with suitcase-loads of baggage — but one look was all it took. She just knew that she and Raoul had to be together.

So the long process of bringing Raoul back from his depression and allowing him to feel safe to express himself started. He was a ball of tension and, when presented with open fields and moorland, was pretty much agoraphobic. He was frightened of everything — if a bucket was moved from its normal place, it was like the end of the world to him. He had been given homoeopathic remedies to try to combat this fear, but this had only served to bring all his fears to the surface. In a way this was positive though as the time was ripe for me to try and help resolve these fears. I have a wonderful homoeopathic vet (her details are in the resource section) who works alongside me as my veterinary advisor. Not all vets are open to this modality, but we feel that it is essential to have choices in the treatment of our animals and that many complementary therapies can definitely aid conventional treatments and contribute to restoring animals' health. I feel that where one course of treatment has not been successful, our animals deserve for us to try to find help for them in any way we can.

When I arrived to see Raoul, he was too afraid to come into the barn because my presence wasn't part of his normal daily routine. Another rescue horse, Vidar, led the way and eventually Raoul was persuaded to come inside and meet me. When I opened my heart to connect with his, I could have burst into tears as I felt the huge well of sadness inside him. I felt that it was incredibly important that he had come to Kate, as her lesson was that she needed to reconnect with nature and learn to notice all the rhythms and nuances of his energy. She told me that she had always loved horses, but her family were not animal-minded and she had lived for a great part of her life in the city, feeling like an alien and not really knowing why.

Raoul telepathically showed me a previous lifetime as a Native American pony with Kate as a young brave. He gave me the most wonderful image of open plains and freedom. I knew that they both had to go back to this lifetime and reconnect with that sense of freedom and fearlessness. He showed me the young man sitting bareback on the black-and-white pony, with his arms outstretched as though saluting the sun in total peace and at one with nature, before they started galloping flat out in gay abandon. I asked Kate to see if she could imagine any images of this lifetime—(I always let the horse show the person what they looked like and when they describe the same thing that the horse has previously shown me, I know we're on the right track). Kate said she was a young man barelegged sitting astride a horse with no saddle and that her mount was black and white. I began to feel excited as I encouraged her to remember how that felt, and she said it gave her the most wonderful sense of peace and freedom. I asked her to imagine breathing that feeling into every cell of her body, and her smile grew bigger and bigger as she was filled with the power of the experience. I asked her to keep visualizing and projecting this image to Raoul so that they could both bring this wonderful energy into their current life together. Raoul then started to give huge yawns, and as his beautiful face contorted we knew he was releasing some of the bottled-up tension and fear from deep inside him. He appeared to be much calmer, and Kate seemed very excited as she reclaimed her oneness with nature. I suggested some Australian Bush Flower essences to complement the session, and waited to hear how Raoul progressed.

This was an unusual case in that Raoul and Kate had to actively go back to their past life to bring back the experience, rather than change it. It was a lifetime of connection, free from limitation. I felt that their lesson in this current incarnation was to overcome their enforced restrictions and disconnection and to rediscover the joy of being completely at one with themselves and the planet.

This was the feedback I received from Kate after my visit.

After you had left on Friday I took the horses down to the field and, as usual, I waited to see how Raoul reacted—quite often, he will go off for a quick sprint or play with his mate Vidar, which is always fun to watch. This time, he set off at a gallop and then turned and galloped back and he did that four times! But that is not all; during one of these sprints, he did something I have never seen from him before. He did the most enormous buck in mid-air so that all four feet were off the ground and his hind legs were both straight out behind him just like the Lipizzaner horses do at the Spanish Riding School in Vienna. It was like the most enormous release for him and he looked so happy.

Not only is he happier but so am I! I truly feel like I have found the answer as to why I feel and think the way I do, which is on the whole, different from most people. Instead of feeling that I am odd, I feel that it is right that I should be like this and I feel confident about myself and how I think. So I thank you for that.

I am trying to do a lot more visualization. When the boys are in the barn Raoul tends to fidget more than the others, so when I was in there last I stood near him and tried to visualize him in the correct position, as he was facing the wrong direction. He did not move at first, but immediately I began visualizing him where I wanted him to be, Vidar nudged Raoul on the bum as if to say 'Do as she asks' and Raoul promptly moved into the correct position. I don't know whether that was coincidence but it was amazing.

Maybe it is the difference in me but, only this morning, Raoul walked past a very scary thing with me for the first time—before he would just panic and turn around. I definitely feel a sense of calm and confidence that has eluded me before and I am sure that it is all down to you!

Kate

Personally, I feel that it's down to Raoul choosing to come back to Kate to help reconnect them both. Aren't animals amzing?

CHAPTER 2

Are animals always the same species in a past life?

W hen I first started working with horses, my experience was nearly always that they had been within the equine family in their past incarnations. Not necessarily as a horse, though—I saw mules and zebras, and even a tiny multi-toed Eohippus, the first ancestor of the horse we know today. I assumed that this was the same with all species, and only wondered when I was told by my vet friend that they were sure the new puppy that a family had just acquired was the reincarnation of a foal that they had lost recently. This was still new territory for me, and at first I was a little sceptical. The horses then obviously decided it was time to educate me; during a demonstration in front of a group of students, the mare I was working with announced that she had been a master of Eastern medicine in a past life—meaning that she had been human before! This took a bit of getting my head round, as you can imagine. After accepting that this concept could indeed be possible, all sorts of incredible cases presented themselves to me—cases that furthered my understanding that, on a soul level, we can choose whatever vehicle best suits our needs for the utmost evolution of our souls. The following story was incredible indeed and showed once again how the past can create the root of issues in our current incarnation.

Rowena and Kizzie—Irish Roots

I had a session with a lovely girl called Rowena who had been worried about her cat Kizzie. Kizzie yowled incessantly and, although she did not appear to be nervous as such, seemed to be permanently on edge. She also stared at Rowena, as if she were trying to tell her something and hoping that if she yowled long and loud enough, Rowena might get the message.

As Rowena seated herself in my healing room, true to form, Kizzie was yowling loudly from her basket on the floor. I noted that Rowena was quite thin, and she admitted to also always feeling on edge, as though there was always the possibility of some impending disaster. Rowena also told me that she had a son who she also felt very anxious about, and that she never managed to fully switch off her inexplicable fear. I thought that perhaps Kizzie was trying to help heal Rowena's anxiety and had resorted to making her dreadful din to force Rowena to seek help so that the issues could be finally resolved. We decided to let Kizzie out of her basket, whereupon she calmly positioned herself in front of Rowena and stared up as though willing us to understand what was going on. I immediately got a picture in my mind of a poor family struggling in Ireland during the potato famine. I could see a bedraggled mother with two children kneeling in the earth sobbing. They were all painfully thin. Kizzie 'told' me that she was Rowena's brother in this past life and that James, Rowena's son in her current life, was her mother! I wasn't sure how Rowena would respond to this and was wondering how to broach the subject when Rowena suddenly said "I think Kizzie was there as a human and I think James was there too." It seemed appropriate to ask her to picture what might have happened and when I did, to my amazement, she 'saw' exactly what Kizzie had shown me. However, the more she described the family's terrible plight the more she felt her throat constricting and, when I asked her what it felt like, she said it felt like lumps—great lumps of grief. Through her tears she described how they had all died. I asked how Kizzie might help us change this awful outcome. Kizzie was still sitting stock-still, directing us, and was completely silent—which was a first! I got a picture in my head of the family all praying and trying to dance a fertility dance. There was a beautiful aura of love pervading the family as they hugged each other. I suggested that Rowena might also picture this and see if she could really feel the love. The images came flooding into her mind easily and she said she could then visualize the crop thriving and that they all survived. As she did this, she reported the lumpy feeling in her throat completely disappearing and said she felt a huge feeling of relief. She had never been able to eat well and had always worried about whether there would be enough, even though in this life her family were by no means poor. She also said that although James was still very young, he always seemed very sensible and an 'old soul' and was very protective of her. Rowena, who had no trace of an accent, then told me that her family came from Ireland!

29

Roma's Story

This is an in-her-own-words account by Pam, the owner of German Shepherd dog Roma, of their amazing journey together through time.

This is the story of my beautiful dog Roma, a six-year-old German Shepherd, who moved to France with me and my other dog when we left Africa two years ago.

Last year I asked Madeleine for a reading from Roma, who has had a major problem with aggression towards all other animals ever since the first one she saw when she was about four months old. I have never got the impression that she wanted a fight; she just seems to want to scare them away and, unfortunately, she has always been very efficient at it. I am a very competent dog owner and trainer and I had tried all sorts of things to help, from head collars to flower essences and food supplements, but they made no difference. We were both going round and round in circles and only getting worse. However, ever since I had solved some problems of my own using past-life regression, I had begun to think more about past lives and thought that there might be something in a past life of mine that was impacting on both me and Roma, so I sent a photo and hair sample to Madeleine.

Madeleine's reading said that all she could see when she looked at us were lions. She thought that in a past life I had been Roma's cub and that Roma had failed to protect me from a marauding male lion; she had felt devastated when she lost me and thought that she had failed. Consequently, in this life she is in overdrive to make sure it doesn't happen again. I have to say that when I read this I thought, 'Oh no, what on earth have I got myself into here with a crackpot of a woman!' I replied that Roma had been born in Kenya, and I didn't have a problem with the idea of her having previously been a lion, but I didn't think that humans came back as animals and I had trouble with the lion-cub part. I added though that Roma certainly did go into overdrive whenever she saw another animal.

Madeleine's reply was very detailed. She talked about a previous case of hers where a horse had a past life as a man—a cavalry officer. He had been so disgusted by the carnage inflicted on the horses in his charge that he had reincarnated as a horse several times in order to experience the same fate. Madeleine explained that she believes we can choose how we wish to incarnate to suit our soul lessons. This explanation made me feel a lot happier, and I started Roma and myself on the Bach flower essence Honeysuckle, suggested by Madeleine as it can help with letting go of the past.

Several days later I decided to give Roma some Reiki, and during the session I started to feel some emotion and wasn't sure where it was coming from. I also had a mental picture of a lioness carrying a cub in her mouth and could feel a great deal of love and emotion for the lioness. I was also feeling anger, so I meditated and managed to release the emotion. I am sure it was anger about my life as a lion being cut short. I was in floods of tears when I finished, and Roma, who hadn't moved a muscle since her Reiki session, let out a huge sigh.

Roma's eyes

I still wasn't sure, though, about having been a lion, so I wrote to a psychic who has given me lots of help in the past and asked her if she had ever been aware of any lions around me. She wrote back saying no, but weirdly she had been drawing lions all week, and tuning into my energy she could feel that I had recently done a very positive release. This proved to me that I had obviously not imagined the lion release I had just done.

I now had much more confidence that it was not just my imagination and that Madeleine was not a crackpot, so a few days later I decided to take it further and see if I could step into the life of the lion cub. I found that I could; it was not difficult. I saw what looked like the East Africa plains and three lion cubs playing on a *kopje* (rocky outcrop) in what I think was the Serengeti, which is a place that I inexplicably always avoided visiting. I saw that I had two lion cub brothers, but they had died. In this life my family and I went through a time of great hardship and drought, with barren land and carcasses of animals and no water or food. My brothers died because their mother, Roma, had not been able to feed and water them. I didn't see how I died but what I did feel was the most unbearable grief, pain and anguish from Roma. This must have been a dreadful life for Roma and I realized that it had to be me who helped her to release it, but I didn't know how to.

Madeleine's planned visit to France came a week after Roma's seventh birthday, when she came to meet us. She noted that Roma was constantly on alert and seemed to be doing 'risk assessment' the whole time, and that she still carried a lot of grief from her life as a lion. She also noted how powerful Roma's eyes are—she has a menacing and penetrating stare. Madeleine also felt that Roma's soul chakras were blocked, and did an unblocking exercise on them. When Roma was ready, Madeleine asked me to open a heart connection with her and took me back to being a lion cub, with the intention of rewriting what had happened so that this time it had a happy ending. When the male lion appeared Roma hid me in a crack underneath the kopje and went down the path to meet him. Although she was very weak she tried to appear strong and the lion decided not to interact with her, instead walking in another direction. Roma sat and watched while he moved away, making sure that he had completely gone, and as she sat it started to rain. Big drops of sparkling rain fell from a thundery sky, and the air was full of the smell of the rain that signified the end of the drought and renewed the land. My next picture was of a young lioness with her mother, fit and healthy, glowing with strength and power, surveying the plains from their kopje. In a fresh and green land they went hunting together, each complementing the other and forming a good team. This is the picture that I still carry with me now—their strength, vitality, empowerment and unity.

Empowerment is not just for Roma but also for me; the success of this treatment, I realized, depends on me being able to tap into my lion empowerment when I need to.

To help cement this into place and to make sure all the negative karmic cords were cut, Madeleine also suggested that we both take the Australian bush flower essence Boab, an extremely powerful essence that releases negative thought patterns, experiences and deeply held emotions, particularly around family.

A couple of days after we had seen Madeleine, Roma and I were in the car and I stopped to chat to a friend, who put his head close to the window. This would normally be a cue for Roma to start barking and shaking all over, but this time, I realized, she was looking calm and uninterested. Even my friend commented on it; in fact, he actually thought she was my other dog because her behaviour was so different. I can't express the boost that this gave me, and how much it made me believe that everything was going to be all right.

In fact, I was feeling so confident that I arranged to meet a friend who had two small dogs and for all of us, including my other dog, to go for a walk together. I meditated a few days before we met and got a picture of Roma walking along a track in front of us with the other dogs. The image was very vivid and I tried hard to hold on to it. When I let Roma out of the car on the day, she did all her usual stuff and dragged me across the road to see the other dogs, and my heart fell. After about five minutes, though, Roma started to calm down. She had never been this good before and I started feeling better. During our walk I let Roma off the lead and, although she wasn't particularly friendly towards the other dogs, she didn't do any damage; when she was coming on too strongly they told her off and she would back off. After about twenty minutes I realized that she had settled down completely, and saw in real life the picture that I had received during my meditation. Several weeks later, and I am trying to be brave and let Roma off the lead to deal with other animals herself as she is definitely better if she is loose. I have realized that I stand a better chance of being calm when I am not being dragged around on the end of the lead. I just need to have good judgement about which dogs will be OK to let her loose with. We have recently been on a walk with six other dogs, during which Roma's behaviour was fine. She still gives other animals the eye, but the intensity is no longer there and her body language is different, plus, importantly, I am different—I am not as worked up, worried or panicky. Flower essences often work very subtly and it is easy to think they don't make a difference, as I did when Roma and I started taking Boab. However, now I look back and see how much calmer I am with Roma, I think taking Boab has helped. I have realized that I have always worried that Roma, or another animal, or I, would be hurt; however, these fears are quite ungrounded, I know now, as nothing bad has ever happened in this lifetime. All that my worrying has done is make Roma's behaviour worse, as she has tried to protect me. I suspect that we have had several past lives together that have not ended happily. However, now that I am fully aware of all this it is easier to deal with as it has changed my life. Anyone with an aggressive dog will know how carefully walks have to be planned, how hard you have to work to avoid certain places, people, times and animals, and also how embarrassed and inadequate it makes you feel as an owner. In the end, the question of whether or not Roma and I really used to be lions doesn't really matter; it is the rewriting of the script and the work I did with Madeleine that has given me new confidence and calm.

Roma and I are building up our socializing with other animals gradually as I don't want to rush it and spoil our progress, but there is no reason now why the story should not have a happy ending.

Roma on her walk

Roma also facilitated another past-life healing for Pam, who had been struggling with a condition where she didn't have any sensations or strength in her hands. This was obviously bad for her work as a Reiki healer. When I visited them in France and we released the 'lion' life trauma, Roma also wanted me to help Pam further her career as a healer. She showed me a lifetime where Pam had been a young girl in medieval France. She had been a very gifted healer, but of course in that time there was much suspicion and prejudice and she had to take great care not to be labelled as a witch. Pam was called to help a little girl who was very sick with consumption. The girl was the daughter of a nobleman who was desperate and would do anything to save his child's life. Pam entered the magnificent castle and was ushered into the darkened room where the pallid child lay. The nobleman begged her to save the girl and Pam tried her best, but the girl deteriorated and died. The man flew into a fury and blamed Pam. He ordered one of his henchmen to chop off both of Pam's hands, and she was thrown out of the castle. She died from her wounds in that lifetime, the trauma of which has made her in this lifetime very unsure about her healing abilities. Pam had always been very hesitant about even discussing her desire to give healing and had kept it a secret from her family. This all came to light when Roma requested that I ask Pam about her hands. Pam said that she had been suffering with a little arthritis, particularly in her left hand. As I studied her hands I was puzzled to 'see' a sort of line across each wrist that looked like a very faint scar. It almost looked as though her hands had been stuck back on. Roma sat next to us and 'fed' me the pictures of what had transpired and I relayed them to Pam, wondering again what she would make of my findings! However, she was used to my rather strange way of intuiting by now and she totally trusted Roma's judgement. With Roma's help we went back to Pam's past life to change the outcome; this time, Pam visualized the child being filled with light from her hands and brimming with renewed health. The nobleman was so grateful that he showered Pam with gifts and, for the rest of her life, supported and protected her. Her gifts were celebrated and she was much revered. In this lifetime, as the exercise started working, energy started to flood into Pam's hands and she felt a renewed excitement at the potential she now felt she had to help others.

It was very important for Roma to witness Pam being re-empowered. I emphasized the importance of them hunting as a team—Roma as the old lioness, using her life experience, and Pam using her youth and agility to make the kills. Together as a unit they would aid the pride's survival. It was wonderful to see Roma's eyes, previously extremely piercing and not a little daunting, soften. She was a very dominant bitch and it was easy to see how she might have been previously a very threatening lioness. Her grief at her inability to save her cub had made her overprotective in her current life with Pam, but she had chosen to reconnect with her in this lifetime so that all the grief could be healed at last and they could both begin to enjoy their lives together fully.

Claire and Bess — Visit from the Other Side

You're damned if you do and damned if you don't. You're always consumed with guilt to the point that random acts of kindness leave you plagued with doubt. Should you have tried to help, or did your suggestion cause a problem that wouldn't have happened otherwise? You become full of self-doubt and this impinges on every area of your life. You might become obsessive or even not want to speak to people at all for fear you'll say the wrong thing and trigger the wrong chain of events. Whatever you do it never seems to cause the right outcome.

Claire was a person who felt that anything that happened, however random, had to be her fault. She blamed herself for anything that befell her family or pets and she would contrive a belief that it had to have been because of her. For example, she suggested to her daughter that she should make regular checks on herself because of a history of breast cancer in the family. She then read that our beliefs create our reality, and decided that she had 'made' her daughter think about getting breast cancer and that now she would and it would all be her fault. In this case, Claire was quite reassured by my suggestion that, in fact, she was just being a caring parent, and that surely she would feel worse if she hadn't suggested that her daughter check herself and she'd found out too late that there was a problem.

Claire came to one of my animal communication workshops. She seemed to participate and contribute well and her intuitive skills were definitely expanding as she grew in confidence. However, when we came to work on the photographs and hair samples of the animals that the participants had brought in, it became obvious that Claire had some very deep issues that needed to be released and healed. She'd booked to have a reading with me to see if I could 'tune in' to her beloved Bess, a springer spaniel who'd passed earlier that year. Claire duly arrived at my home protectively clutching her handbag, which I discovered contained a box of ashes and some well-thumbed photos of her lovely dog. She was very emotional, understandably. Any animal lover will tell you how devastating it is to be separated from your animal companion, and the suffering one experiences in trying to cope with grief. I soon discovered, though, that there was much more to it than that.

There was such a plethora of roller coaster emotions intertwined and feeding each other, but the overriding, all-consuming, crippling and most debilitating one was guilt. Claire seemed to be completely racked, consumed and even obsessed with the thought pattern that everything that had happened to Bess was her fault. As I gently held Bess's picture, I gazed down at a very typical, bouncy, vivacious springer spaniel with endless energy and joie de vivre. She came bounding into my thoughts and obviously wanted to help Claire big time. With Bess's help I soon realized that there was much more going on here than straightforward grief. Bess announced, in a very matter-of-fact way, that Claire felt guilty about everything and was punishing herself mercilessly. I gently questioned Claire to see if she understood what Bess was referring to, and she instantly burst into tears. Everything seemed at first to stem from an incident when Claire was quite young, when she'd experienced a very mild falling-out with a friend, who soon afterwards had been killed in a car accident. Claire immediately blamed herself and felt responsible, and developed OCD (obsessive-compulsive disorder). She became fanatical about checking and re-checking everything and her obsessions started to make her ill. However, she was told by her mother that she had to stop this behaviour as it was making her (Claire's mother) ill. Rather than making her 'snap out of it', this approach only served to make Claire internalize all her fears and self-loathing, and feel even more guilty for making her mother ill. She felt unable to confide in anyone about her difficulties.

Claire then admitted that she had developed ME at the same time and had been struggling with this debilitating condition ever since. I could 'see' Bess sitting on Claire's lap trying to give her healing into her solar plexus, the energy centre that impacts on our self-worth and sense of self. If there is a lack of energy flow to this abdominal region, there will be physical and emotional consequences. Bess asked me to ask Claire about her digestive system and to question her as to whether she'd had an upset stomach, and if Claire held tension in that area. Claire confirmed that she'd been suffering from an upset stomach for the previous few days and was indeed rather fragile that morning too. I explained that Bess was trying to give her solar plexus a lovely energy boost, and Claire began to feel warmth in that area and a slight pressure on her lap. I suggested that Claire allow Bess to continue giving her healing help when she could find a quiet time at home, by sitting or lying and visualizing Bess's soft warm body cuddling her, and Bess confirmed that she was definitely up for the task. I told Claire that I felt that due to the intensity of the challenges she was experiencing there was a past-life issue impacting on her present life. Claire said that a hypnotherapist had told her the same thing, but that she had not had the courage to return to investigate it further. I felt that Bess was desperate to help Claire resolve this once and for all after their life together and that all she wanted was for her human companion to be healed. Fortunately, I received a phone call from Claire a week later asking to make an appointment. I could feel Bess's excitement and see a very wiggly bottom as she frantically wagged her stumpy tail with joy.

Claire was feeling some trepidation as to what was going to unfold during the session, but her fears were soon allayed as she felt Bess sitting next to her, and reached down with her hand as she said she could feel Bess's lovely floppy, soft ears. She even felt Bess leaning against her legs. Her presence was so real that I almost felt I'd have to hoover the carpet afterwards to remove the brown and white hairs!

With Bess presiding and overseeing the proceedings, Claire felt much more at ease, and I gently probed and encouraged her to divulge a little more about her past. Claire admitted that she was still punishing herself for what she perceived had been rough treatment of Bess—she had once pulled her off a chair to put her outside for a pee. Bess was quite elderly and had become rather stiff and creaky by then and had been slow in her responses, which could be frustrating to the fraught and extremely pressurized Claire. Bess was amazed that Claire had interpreted the incident so harshly and felt no resentment whatsoever. However, this did nothing to comfort Claire, who then went on to say that towards the end of Bess's life she'd tried to place a cool compress on an inflamed part of the dog's leg, and felt that Bess must have caught a chill from the compress and Claire had somehow been responsible for Bess's death. This was quite clearly not the case, and we discussed the possibility that perhaps Bess had actually gained some relief from the compress, but I could tell that Claire wasn't convinced. Her logical mind did see the logic, but her old patterning wouldn't allow her any reprieve.

Claire admitted that she'd suffered post-natal depression and had been terrified in case something awful should befall her children. She had even attempted suicide once, as she'd felt that everyone would be far better off without her. Her guilt issues were in danger of devouring her, but I felt that Bess was not going to allow that to happen. I placed a couple of aura-cleansing drops in Claire's hands and asked her to rub her hands together and breathe in the aroma. I use these 'Protector' drops for all my clients—horses especially love them.

I asked Claire to visualize the healing effect of the drops and she pictured little balls of sunshine flowing around her body as she breathed in the little molecules of gentle strength and calm. When the balls of sunshine were taking effect, Bess guided me to help Claire perform some deep healing on her emotional heart. I will discuss the technique for this powerful healing visualization in the self-help chapter later. When I asked Claire to visualize her heart in front of her, she tearfully exclaimed that it was all blue and black. I suggested that perhaps it was symbolically 'black and blue' due to the bruising it had suffered emotionally, to which Claire agreed. There also appeared to be a steel casing surrounding her heart, which she felt had been there at one time to protect it, but which was now restricting and constricting it. With Bess's help, Claire managed to visualize removing the casing, which took a lot of courage as it allowed the symbolic heart to be very exposed and vulnerable. I asked Claire how her heart felt and she said just one word: 'devastated'. I then asked Claire to visualize going into her heart in order to symbolically facilitate healing from the inside out. She said it was very dark so she imagined having some kind of sci-fi laser beam to burn through the darkness. She imagined opening windows and letting the sunshine in. She filled her heart with sunshine and lit aromatic candles to create a very beautiful, light space. She felt very happy with the new feeling inside her heart, so she then imagined being back outside and saw her heart now glowing with life and light—a very different image from the poor damaged thing she had previously visualized. I asked her how it felt now and she said, "Calmer and more at peace." I asked her to place the heart back in her chest and to notice how it felt inside her body. She said that she could feel her whole body beginning to respond to the glowing, sunshine energy of her newly healed heart. I asked her to imagine every cell glowing with sunshine as she reclaimed her power, and we finished the exercise by wrapping the whole of her body in sunshine. Bess was once again ecstatic with joy as she witnessed the healing for her human friend. I felt that Claire had worked hard enough for that session and had been incredibly courageous in being willing to address her issues. I felt that we needed to perform this exercise before we addressed the distressing experiences from her past life that had so damaged her self-belief.

In the next session, I again saw Bess march in determinedly at Claire's side. I almost felt I had to provide a bowl of water along with Claire's cup of tea! I asked Claire's permission to delve into the past-life scenario that was the root cause for her trauma, and with Bess's help I tuned in. I was shown a life where Claire was living in Poland. She was Jewish, and because of her race both she and her children were in mortal danger from the Nazis. Her terrified family had been in hiding in a war-torn old apartment building and had thus far escaped discovery, but they had just been informed that the buildings in that street were going to be thoroughly searched in a radical 'cleansing' of the area. Claire had received word of an offer of escape to the country, but she had to get her children out at the appointed hour in order to meet her rescuers. I 'saw' her trying to wake her children in the middle of the night. Her daughter did not want to stir from her warm bed and Claire had to forcibly pull her child up. I realized with a shock of recognition that this was mirrored in Claire's current life when she had been filled with guilt about pulling Bess from her chair. I just had this deep feeling of 'knowing' that Bess had been Claire's daughter in that past life. This explained the intensity of their relationship. Unfortunately, their departure was discovered due to a minute detail that Claire had overlooked—she had left a small powdering of dust from some wooden panels that she had hurriedly replaced in her desperation to leave. No sooner had Claire and her family vacated the building than a soldier with a flashlight who was patrolling the area decided to inspect the building. He noticed the errant dust and rushed outside to see the disappearing silhouettes of the woman and her two children. Tragically, they were sprayed with gunfire and all perished. Claire's dying thought was, 'It's all my fault! My children have died because of me!'

This explained the extreme intensity of the guilt that Claire felt about everything. With past-life trauma, a person can come into their current life with an underlying issue that is then triggered by what might seem like an insignificant event or situation, but with cataclysmic results. The problem is that we feel the fear without understanding where it comes from. Once the root cause of the fear is accessed, it can be released and understanding and healing can take place. This is why Claire, in this life, felt such terror that something awful might happen to her children without knowing why. How amazing to think that Bess had chosen to incarnate as a dog this time to help resolve the trauma and also to facilitate Claire's healing. The depth of love between them was extraordinary, and it had taken Bess's death in this lifetime to finally get to the bottom of the problem. It may seem that incarnating as an animal might appear to be a 'backward step' in a person's spiritual evolution, but I would argue that there is no better way to resolve a trauma or to give healing and companionship to a human, than to be a soft furry creature that can give unconditional love.

Claire became quite distressed as I gently relayed the most delicate version of her past life that I could compose. She still felt dreadful and blamed herself totally; she thought that her failure to notice the dust was stupid. This helped to explain her OCD; she had to constantly check minutiae as she thought that if she missed something, however small, there would be terrible consequences. She could now understand this and I suggested that at least she had been giving her children some glimmer of hope that they would escape, whereas if they had remained in the building they would have had no chance at all. It was pure bad luck that the soldier had appeared at that time and most definitely not Claire's fault. I do believe that we can choose our life's paths and that everything happens for a reason in order for us to gain the most learning we can on our soul's journey. But this was a very hard lesson and it proved to me that, on a soul level, Claire was an extremely strong and evolved being—she would have to be in order to have chosen such a severe task. The weight of self-punishment was, however, currently physically and emotionally crippling her.

To finally work through this and to help Claire heal, I used some NLP (neurolinguistic programming) techniques that are very useful for externalizing a person's emotional pain. I asked Claire to visualize an image that represented her at this moment in time. It could be an animal, bird or an object. She chose a rabbit. I asked her where the rabbit was, what sex it was and how it felt. She said it was in a field, it was female and it was feeling vulnerable. I asked why and she said it was worried about being shot. I then asked her to visualize a future image, which represented her as the person who had let go of all her fears and guilt and had completely forgiven herself for all her perceived failings. This time she chose a giraffe, as it had a tall overview of every situation and was full of grace and serenity. Again it was a female, who felt very peaceful and happy, completely knowing who she was. I asked the giraffe to 'talk' to the rabbit and give advice as to how to release her fears and become happy. When clients are doing this, I ask them to place one image in each hand and allow dialogue to flow between them, as this allows each image to express itself and the future image to help the current image to grow into its positive, healed future self. Eventually, as the client moves through the exercise, the two hands meet and integrate with each other. The giraffe advised the rabbit to just keep going and she would find that she would lose her fear, that she should recognize all the skills that she had developed through being a prey animal and appreciate all her keen senses and survival instincts. Claire's hands met each other and her images became a beautiful pink orb of strength that could then be absorbed into her heart and from there into every cell of her body, allowing a shift of self-belief pattern into a more positive and manageable state of being.

I then used a wonderful technique that was shown to me by a lovely friend, Thea, when she helped train me; a technique that acts as an instant barometer of our chakra energies. The chakras are centres of energy within our body that connect not only to physiological systems within us but also to our emotions. In order to achieve physical and emotional well-being there must be a strong flow of energy through each centre to bring about optimum health.

Tillie / Bess

Claire left the session feeling invigorated and Bess continued to give her loving support. I marvelled yet again at the level of commitment between soulmates, be they human or animal.

The latest update I have had from Claire is an email with a photograph attached of a new spaniel puppy, Tillie. Her adorable eyes gazed out from the screen and I could see Bess shining out at me. Bess had returned, again as a dog, to continue her loving support for Claire. I was so glad that Claire had overcome her issues of guilt and concern and the weight of responsibility. I knew that she had wanted to feel confident enough to take on another puppy, but hadn't previously believed she could cope. Here was living proof of her progress, and I was so thrilled for her and Tillie.

The chakra technique Claire and I used harnesses the power of imagery and the self-healing abilities of the mind to immediately facilitate healing change deep within us. The more we can practise this technique, the easier it becomes to perform a quick check on what is going on.

There are many other chakras both within and around us, but the seven described here are the basic or main ones, and can be worked on with very revealing and powerful results. Our animals have similar chakra centres in their body and with practice, you can also intuit similar images and transformation for them.

The Chakra Systems

Base chakra	Located at the base of the spine. Associated with the colour red and the element of earth. SENSE: Smell. EMOTION(S): Acceptance, stability, grounding and survival.
Sacral chakra	Located within the pelvis. Associated with the colour orange and the element of water. SENSE: Taste. Connected to the kidneys, adrenals, reproductive system and lymphatic system. EMOTION(S): Identity and validation.
Solar plexus chakra	Located above the navel. Associated with the colour yellow and the element of fire. SENSE: Sight. Connected to the digestive system, liver and stomach. EMOTION(S): Self-worth issues.

Heart chakra	Located over the chest area and in between the shoulder blades. Associated with the colours green and pink, and the element of air. SENSE: Feel/touch. Connected to the thymus gland, heart and lungs. EMOTION(S): Self-love.
Throat chakra	Located in the throat area. Associated with the colour blue and the element of the heavens. SENSE: Hearing. Connected to the thyroid gland, throat, ears, nose and mouth. EMOTION(S): Self-expression.
Third eye/brow chakra	Located in the centre of the forehead. Associated with the colour indigo and the element silver. SENSE: Inner knowledge. Associated with and connected to the pineal gland, sleep and wake states and the brain. EMOTION(S): Self-awareness/intuition.
Crown chakra	Located on top of the head. Associated with the colour Violet and the element gold. SENSE: Thought and connection to the divine. Associated with the pituitary gland, craniosacral system, central nervous system, hair and the skin. EMOTION(S): Spiritual/personal power.

When Claire and I examined each chakra centre, we invited an image to form to represent what was going on energetically in each area, emotionally and physically. Any perceived negative image can then be transmuted by visualizing white light pouring in from the Universe and transforming the image into something very beautiful and more positive. Images are very personal and vary from individual to individual, but below I describe what Claire visualized.

Base Chakra

A golf ball. I thought this was a rather hard image, so I asked Claire to imagine bringing beautiful white light down through her body and blasting the golf ball with it until it became something she could feel happier about. The white light melted the ball and it became a crystalline white light energy, which was her foundation.

Sacral chakra

A beautiful pair of wings. As this represented Claire's identity and her feelings about being a woman, she was very happy with this image.

Solar plexus chakra

A beautiful purple blanket. Claire felt very comfortable with this image, so again we happily left it unchanged.

Heart chakra

An orange. This had to be opened so that the segments could unfold—which I thought was a very positive image to show Claire's willingness to open her heart!

Throat chakra

Barbed wire and a tight and constricted feeling. As this is the site of self-expression, Claire and I felt the need for a zap of white light. This then transmuted into a beautiful pink swirl, which I felt represented 'speaking from her heart' as pink is the heart colour.

Third eye/brow chakra

A beautiful starry sky. Claire seemed very happy with this image.

Crown chakra

Here Claire visualized a craggy crater. She decided that she would fill it with white light until it was full up. Once this was accomplished the crater had a beautiful lush green top and she felt much more positive about the feeling of the image. We discussed the symbolism of being filled up or full, or even fulfilled, which resonated very strongly with Claire.

Josephine and Beetle — A Stormy Night

The following case shows that it is not only humans who can carry guilt — this little dog felt he had a lot to prove in his current incarnation! This is the story of a tiny terrier who had tried without success to save his human friend in a past life. He was determined to make absolutely sure that she was safe in this lifetime.

"None of us are getting any sleep. We're getting desperate. Please help!" Josephine pleaded on the phone in an exasperated tone. She went on to explain that she'd recently married and that at first everything had been going well in the relationship between her new husband and their little dog, until a violent storm one night. Ever since then their nights had been constantly disrupted. Beetle, the terrier, had found it impossible to remain downstairs alone, and had created such a commotion that the only way his owners could get any rest was to allow him into their bedroom for the night. I started by attempting distance work to release his fear of storms, but to no avail. Beetle remained just as distressed –in fact his behaviour seemed to be worsening.

When I arrived at Josephine's house, I was greeted by a black-and-tan tornado who whizzed between my legs, frantically checking and sniffing me to determine if I was friend or foe. Once he had ascertained that I was probably there for legitimate reasons, I was ushered into the living room by beetle. The diminutive dog sat at my feet, fixing me with a very determined stare. I gently coaxed him, telepathically, to try to explain his anxiety, and reassured him that I'd do my utmost to help. I questioned him about his fears connected to the storm and what he showed me, in a video-like clip, was rather disturbing. I saw Josephine being assaulted. I tried to find out from her if she'd ever had any difficult relationships where she might have felt threatened sexually. She replied that this had never been the case, so I questioned Beetle further. He then took me through their past-life trauma, where Josephine had been a teenage girl from a very poor family who lived in a log cabin in what looked like a North American forest. He showed me the girl dressed in a shabby cotton dress and with unkempt hair.

One night a violent storm had raged and a stranger had arrived at their door and been allowed in to shelter for the night. Beetle showed me that in that incarnation, he had been an old yellow hound who loved his family fiercely, especially Josephine, as they'd grown up together. He'd been very reluctant to allow the strange dishevelled man into the house, but Josephine's kindly parents had felt sorry for the drenched man, allowing him respite from the elements and shutting the dog in an outhouse so that the man could warm and dry himself by the fire that burned brightly in the living quarters. When everyone was asleep the man had crept into Josephine's sleeping quarters, which were separate from her parents'. He threatened her with a knife so that she would keep quiet while he assaulted her. Beetle felt her anxiety and started to howl, trying to alert the family. Unfortunately, he was shouted at and then ignored, so poor Josephine just had to endure the awful experience. The man ran off before Josephine could cry for help and poor Beetle never forgave himself for not being able to save his friend.

This was obviously a very difficult subject to raise, but I knew that we had to address it so that the underlying trauma could be released and healed. Beetle had remained motionless at my feet while he relayed the account I heard in my head. Josephine commented on his unusual stillness and fixed expression and intuited that he seemed to be telling me something. Poor Beetle, he was very upset that he couldn't prevent his friend's past dishonour and he felt that he had failed her. The storm had triggered the past-life memory, and it had combined with the fact that Josephine was now married. Even though Beetle was very attached to Josephine's husband, he was still distraught at not being able to monitor and protect his owner in her current life, and felt that if he could be with them at night, he would be able to ensure that all was well.

I conveyed all that Beetle had told me, and Josephine began to feel quite fearful, as though the deep memory was surfacing. Beetle immediately went and sat at her feet to give her his support. We decided that the best course of action would be to imagine going back in time but, this time, allow the dog to be heard and the stranger thrown out with the help of her father's shotgun before anything untoward happened. Josephine was amazed at her ability to capture the images and emotions as Beetle and I gently helped her through the healing process. Once the change of outcome had taken place, Beetle became extremely animated—he leapt about with a gleeful expression and we laughed at the change in his energy as he frolicked around the room with joy. This did much to lift the tension and lighten the mood and we marvelled at this little dog's courage and sense of commitment to undo a crime.

I was thrilled to hear later on that, from then on, Beetle was content to sleep downstairs, even in rough weather, and that everyone in the household was managing to get their well-deserved rest.

Sally and Barney the Bear!

Sally requested that I visit her and her golden retriever, Barney.

At Sally's home I was met by the most enormous 'goldie' I've ever seen. His legs were like tree trunks and his paws huge. I couldn't stop the image of him as a bear from penetrating my thoughts, and this was before I was almost flattened under the gigantic dog's weight! Fortunately he was a real softie, but the poor thing—barely out of puppyhood, despite his size—had been plagued by illness for all of his short life. He had the most wonderful deep brown eyes, but as I gently gazed at him they began to change. In fact his whole face started to change so that I could see a much darker brown head and golden-coloured circles around his eyes. Sally told me that she too had noticed this and that Barney sometimes seemed to her to look different, especially when he was being fed. He'd contracted some very rare parasites as a young pup and had developed a form of arthritis from the side effects of the drugs he'd been given. He'd been struggling to move properly and had been in some pain. As he gazed up at me—or more accurately as he stared at me nose to nose—I saw him as a huge bear, chained and baited to dance. The location felt like a place somewhere on the Tibet/China border, with people who resembled Mongolians. Barney then showed me Sally, in this previous life a little boy who would steal food and throw it to the bear in secret. The brutish man who owned the bear caught the little boy and beat him, ridiculing him in front of the crowd who gathered to see the bear dance. I asked Sally whether she had ever experienced bullying in her current life as she seemed very content and free from stress. She divulged that her stepfather had been a real brute and had teased her and crushed her self-esteem mercilessly when she was a child. I described what I was seeing from Barney, and Sally felt that the man with the bear was definitely her current stepfather. He had died a couple of years before and, interestingly, Sally said that he had come through from the spirit world to apologize for his treatment of her, at the time when Sally had acquired Barney. We decided to go back and rewrite the script, as Barney 'showed' me that the little boy had been too frightened to go back to feed the bear again and had always felt that he had failed him. Sally admitted that she had despaired of ever being able to help Barney live a happy, pain-free life and had even wondered whether it might be kinder to have him put down, but something always made her feel that she wanted to fight for his life and never give up on him.

Sally rewrote her script by visualizing stealing the bear in the dead of night and running away to a village far away, where they found help. The cruel man was drowned in a flash flood as he chased after them. The bear and the boy lived out the rest of their lives in the forest together, happy. Sally had a huge pain in her heart at the beginning of the session, but when we created the new 'happy ending' the pain completely vanished.

I referred Barney and Sally to a holistic vet friend who is very open to the idea of past-life healing, as I felt that Barney's physical needs would benefit from homoeopathy. Sally didn't tell the vet about the strange past life that had unfolded, in case she was thought a little strange, but my friend picked up on his 'bear' energy straight away and prescribed the homoeopathic remedy bear's milk. The last I heard, both Sally and Barney were doing very well and Barney's health was going from strength to strength.

Pippa and Big Guy — Empowerment

I often perform distance readings for clients who live too far away for a visit. I can work from photographs and hair samples and I am often amazed at the information the animals send me through these materials — especially when the owners find that it resonates with them on profound levels. This is a reading I performed for a lovely lady called Pippa and her cat Big Fella who came through from spirit. Like many people, Pippa was very curious to find out what she needed to learn about their connection and whether she had managed to meet his needs in their life together. Many owners want to know if their pet is safe in spirit, whether they are free from pain and, most often when they have had to put their pet to sleep, if it was the right thing to do and if their pet blamed them in any way. In this case, the cat proved to be a big personality with a lot to say.

Dear Pippa

It's really interesting that you called him Big Fella as he has such a big persona and energy. When I look at his photo and eyes, I get an image of a huge black panther and I am bombarded with knowledge of a previous lifetime in Ethiopia, where you were very high up in a kind of royal family and had him—as a black panther—as your bodyguard. I feel he continued that role in a somewhat more covert, minor way in this lifetime. I was puzzled, as I didn't think black panthers were to be found in Africa but I did some research, which showed that the only African country they *were* found in was Ethiopia. I shouldn't have doubted him! The black panther energy is a very important energy for walking between the two worlds of light and dark, and these animals transmute a lot of negative energy into positive in their spiritual roles. This seems to be a task they have committed to perform from spirit, but they can also do it through a physical being who has the soul wisdom to work with it. He keeps shape-shifting between black panther and his Big Fella domestic cat form as I'm studying his photo—it's quite disconcerting!

I feel you lived quite a precarious life in that time, with much tribal competition and rivalry over the throne and the kingdom, with many invaders, not least the Egyptians trying to raid Ethiopian gold. Gold figures very strongly in that lifetime—it was seen as a magical gift from the gods and was prized for its healing properties as well as its material value. Big Fella, in that lifetime, was a protector and was believed to have mystical powers himself—which of course he did, and still did in this lifetime and continues to do so in spirit.

I feel that his role with you this time round was to help you adapt from being a very big persona in Ethiopia to a lifetime where your presence had to be much more low-key. It's about feeling empowered despite living a more lowly existence. You had huge power and wealth previously and didn't always use that power kindly or wisely—you achieved a sense of power by domination and the subservience of your subjects. Your lesson this time is to feel empowered and good about yourself because of your true authentic essence, rather than the trappings of an inherited way of being. You have had to earn and relearn your self-empowerment and true worth. Big Fella was there to help you on your path of awareness and spiritual reawakening, so this time round you did both have very important roles, just in a much more subtle way.

I feel that the time was right for Big Fella to leave and he feels confident that you have learned well, are much more aware of your strengths and abilities now and are able to move forwards on your spiritual path without him being physically at your side. Are you interested in conservation and big cats in general? I feel that this is a role that Big Fella wants you to get involved with. I feel he may want to come back as a big cat again in 2012, to create healing and awareness. I have recently been working with the white lions in South Africa and they are bringing the healing back to Africa, the place where human existence started. Big Fella is telling me he will be an iconic big cat that you will be drawn to work with, and you will just know him by his eyes. In working together he will be bringing an extra dimension to your work once more.

You have such a deep connection together and your roles are very important. This cat has played a vital role in your life and I will be interested to hear how you feel he has affected you and how your life has changed since knowing him. He is guiding you from spirit now, and you can rest assured that he is there for you and will be back as soon as the time is right and you are ready to step up to the plate in the new way that he described. I hope this resonates with you.

Pippa confirmed her love of big cats and told me that she very much wanted to find a way of working with them at some time in the future.

CHAPTER 3

How can our pets heal us?

Our soul memories comprise our thoughts and perceptions of past events and how they have impacted on us physically and emotionally. Events from our past lives, including of course trauma, are stored in our bodies at a cellular level, but if we can change our thoughts about how something affected us, the trauma can be released. Animals are clever enough to know this, and during an animal communication and healing course I was running, we had some very special help on this front from a beautiful dog called Moriarty. Here is his owner Catherine's story, in her own words, about her feelings and anxieties in their relationship, and how they changed after the group worked to change her thoughts and clear the past.

Moriarty

Moriarty—"Man Who Comes From the Sea"

Moriarty has been in our family for three years, ever since he was old enough to leave his mother. As he grew up, our attachment and our love for each other became more and more intense, to such a level that I constantly lived in fear that he would die and I would be bereft. I even made a plan that when he was five I would get another dog, telling myself that it would be to keep him company but knowing that it would be mainly to lessen my grief when the inevitable happened and Moriarty passed.

Moriarty is an incredible dog, highly intelligent; he is a Border collie and Australian shepherd dog cross and loves to join in with our meditation group and whenever our courses allow him in. He works regularly with Madeleine's animal communication course and is very chatty and friendly with the beginners. After he had been with the group for a morning I was asked to go in and verify the information he had given and discuss our past life together. I have to admit that although I was aware we'd had a past life together, I was not expecting what happened next.

I sat on the sofa and Moriarty sat next to me. He settled down and I put my hand on his shoulder, and the group and Madeleine described a past-life scenario where I was with Moriarty in a Bavarian-type country. Moriarty in this life was an Alsatian dog (a German Shepherd) and I was a man. I fell into a river while crossing a bridge and Moriarty was unable to save me; he waited and waited but obviously I never came back for him. He remembers seeing my hand and sleeve coming out of the water, reaching out to him, but he was unable to reach me and I drowned.

I had a realization at this point that in our current life Moriarty is always holding onto my sleeve and he is very cautious around water—he never goes into even a puddle without checking with us first to make sure it's safe and that we could get him out if he got into trouble.

Madeleine then guided us into a replay where we could change the outcome and I visualized a scenario where I was able to get out of the water; Moriarty was able to get hold of my sleeve and help pull me out, then we got onto the bank and went home, where I dried him and we sat and warmed ourselves in front of the fire. As I narrated this, Moriarty gave a huge sigh and I felt an immense sense of relief.

But that was not all. Madeleine was quite convinced that there was another past-life issue that we also had to resolve—a much earlier life this time, where I was an Inuit living in Alaska. In this life I was a young man with his own sled dogs and a strong will. Moriarty was a husky in this life and was the team's lead dog. We had a great relationship in this lifetime and I relied on him. I had been warned that there was a big storm coming and I shouldn't go out, that the lake was starting to thaw and I should go the long way around, but I was so sure of myself and my dogs that I insisted on going out. There was a girl in another tribe, on the other side of the frozen lake, who I was keen to impress! After I had been to the other encampment and showed off to the girl, I realized that the sky was growing very dark and the storm was approaching faster than I'd thought it would. I took my sled and, believing that we could outrun the storm and get home safely, we raced and raced, the dogs working very hard. When we got to the edge of the lake, the ice was already showing signs of breaking up and as I looked over my shoulder the snow was whipping up. In my stupidity and pride I drove the dogs onto the lake, which was the quickest route back home. I knew the danger, I weighed up the risk, and I failed; halfway across the lake the ice broke and we plunged in, Moriarty in the lead. None of us survived. Moriarty, I discovered, felt responsible for this and has carried this guilt into his current lifetime.

Just as with the previous past life, Madeleine again asked me to meditate on a scenario with a positive outcome, to rewrite the memory and release the guilt. At first I could not imagine any other scenario—it was all so vivid in my mind and no matter how hard I tried I couldn't change that view at the edge of the lake, the fateful decision to cross it, the storm approaching fast and the desperation. I admitted that I was struggling and the rest of the group helped with alternative suggestions, giving me ideas for what could have happened instead. Finally, the right scenario came to my mind.

This time, as I stopped at the side of the lake with the wind whipping the snow up and visibility reducing, Moriarty and the other dogs panting their hearts out, we heard the sounds of another dog team coming round the lake. What a relief! Our village elder, my father, had realized what would happen and brought his sled and team round the lake to meet me. We joined the dog teams together with his team at the front and, with the addition of fresher dogs and the weight of responsibility taken away from me and Moriarty, we sped home ahead of the storm and to safety. This scenario gave me a huge sense of relief and release, and again Moriarty gave a huge sigh as he nestled next to me on the sofa. I also realized with a flood of emotion that the elder, my father in that lifetime, is now the figure who I know in my current life as my spirit guide: his name is Stands with

Bear. It was a great privilege to witness a previous lifetime where my guide was in human form.

   After these experiences there has been a huge change in my feelings for and relationship with Moriarty. I no longer have the terrible irrational fear of him dying and leaving me and he is no longer anxious and clingy with me. It's a much more normal relationship. Of course we love each other as much as we ever did, but there is no disabling fear any more; it's been like untying the apron strings and allowing each other to grow. Thank you Madeleine, and all the people on that animal communication course; it was a priceless experience.

It was obvious to everyone that both Catherine and Moriarty seemed brighter and much more relaxed. We could all see clear images of the terrible fates that befell them in that past life; it was clear that we were being directed by Moriarty, who wanted to remove their guilt and anxiety so that they could relax and enjoy a happy, fun-filled life together. Having been out for a walk with them both near water, I had witnessed Moriarty's caution, but had not realized the extent of Catherine's anxiety at the prospect of anything happening to him. We all dread the time when our pets have to pass, but this was at a level that was affecting their present relationship. Once we tuned in, we could understand why.

Crotchet — A Very Special Rabbit

The following was a reading I performed for a lady called Elizabeth who was devastated at her daughter Caitlin's suicide. The only one to witness this tragedy had been a little house rabbit called Crotchet. Elizabeth wanted to try to make sense of the terrible fate of her daughter and the roles her other animals — Cherry, her dog, and her cat Snoopy, who had both died — had played in their lives. She had suffered in a very abusive marriage and was carrying an incredible weight of guilt over her part in the lives of her children and animals. As we so often see from the information given to us by animals, everything has a purpose, no matter how distressing it may appear on the surface.

Dear Elizabeth,

herewith some information from your pets. They gave me such an overwhelming feeling of love for you — it was very emotional but lovely! Crotchet was such a sweet little soul who tried his best to transmute

Caitlin's pain into something better. He's talking about shame and pressure. Something happened to Caitlin in her past that she felt ashamed of, something that she couldn't talk to you about because she thought it might upset you. She didn't realize that, with how much you loved her, you would have understood and would have forgiven her anything—if indeed there was anything to forgive. Crotchet's role was to support her and 'caretake' her passing—a very special role. It's as if something triggered a vile memory that Caitlin had tried to suppress, but something snapped inside and she felt that she could no longer endure the deceit and pretence to herself. She tried to tell herself that she was a good person (which she was, of course) but there was always an underlying disgust and dissatisfaction with herself. I feel that due to pressure in her childhood, she never felt that she was good enough or achieved enough. I'm sure you would never have made her feel that way, but perhaps there were other people who were hard on her, or she may have experienced peer pressure that she couldn't talk about to you. She could not forgive herself for her perceived failings, and no matter what you or anyone else told her or how much you praised her, she would only have to hear the slightest negative comment to take that to heart instead of the positive comments.

It's interesting that in the photo the earrings that she wore were of masks. I feel that she managed to mask her feelings so well from you that you had no idea of what she was going through. It feels as if Crotchet was her only confidante and the only one privy to those areas of her emotional life. She was such an accomplished person, but something from her past always made it seem that, whatever she achieved, it was never good enough.

Crotchet gave her so much pleasure. He seemed to represent innocence and pure unconditional love, something that she felt only an animal could give without judgement or agendas. I know that's the kind of love that you would have shown her, but there was always an underlying perception of maybe letting you down. Crotchet says that Caitlin chose to experience this difficult life so that she could fully understand and reassure children—especially suicides—of just how much they are loved. In that way she is fulfilling her soul's purpose. In spirit, Caitlin is free and sees the bigger picture of how everything played out—why you had to be with Tom (Elizabeth's former husband) and what you had to learn from him. We choose our parents for what they will teach us in our present incarnation, so that we may continue to evolve on our soul journey.

56

I feel that Cherry is with Caitlin, helping her guide the damaged young souls that come to her. Cherry gives me a great sense of love and compassion. It feels as if she was your canine guardian angel on Earth (which is why she chose you!) and she continues her angelic duties in spirit. She brings a link of love from Caitlin to you. Caitlin knows how difficult and painful it is for you to hear all this, but she hopes that by knowing how important her new role is, it may help just a little. Snoopy (who licks the faces of the children to comfort them) was also a little angel for you and came at a difficult time for you when work was challenging and Tom was very hard on you. We can look back in anger and bitterness, but we have to remember that your marriage and relationship were very important in your evolution as a soul. I think there was unfinished karma from a past life together, so you had to reconnect again in this life in order to have Caitlin and her brother Steve. Snoopy and Cherry chose to be there for you to help you and the children through difficult times and to bring joy to your lives. Cherry is an old soul and I'm sure she has been with you before and will do so again. I'm being shown a grey, rather fluffy cat. I don't know whether you recognize this animal, either now or from the past, but it might possibly be Cherry or Snoopy's new incarnation for when they're ready to come back. Snoopy says that he tried to lick you and transmute all the pressures that you were under in your life—he would scan and remove all that energy that was wearing you out.

I do feel, as was suggested, that Cherry had some kind of embolism to the brain, a sudden pain, but very quick as you say and for her it was the best way to go, with no prolonged pain or suffering. Of course it was just terrible for you left behind, but she wants you to know that she's fine, chasing balls in her spare time and wagging her bottom like mad at you!

I fervently hoped that this would help a little as this poor mother grieved for her dear daughter. Again in this case the animals show how committed they are to supporting us on our soul journeys, however challenging those journeys might be. In Robert Schwartz's book *Your Soul's Plan*, the concept of pre-birth contracts is explained. Understanding this has helped me tremendously in reassuring both myself and other people.

Freddy, Victoria, Rufus and Polly

The following case illustrates just how entwined our lives are with our pets through time and space, and just how much our animals want us to be re-empowered and to be all that we can be.

Freddy

Just before a client, Victoria, was due to come to my house for a healing session, I felt that I had to walk my dogs, Winnie and Teazle, in a nearby wood as I didn't have much time. The dogs seemed to choose the route and near the end of our walk, right in front of me I saw the most perfect white feathers; they looked 'joined' like a pair of wings. It was quite a frosty day and they shone in the sunlight. I marvelled at their beauty and took a couple of steps further, where I found another pair of angelic-looking feather 'wings'. I decided to pick them up and take them home to place on my little altar in my healing room. When Victoria arrived she felt that she had to leave Rufus and Polly, her dogs, in the car whilst we had a discussion about her issues and what she wanted for herself and the dogs that day. I was guided to tell her about the feathers and I was then 'told' that I had to do some sound healing with my crystal bowl to remove negative ties. As I seated myself on the floor in readiness to play the bowl I felt large hands on my shoulders, as though they were directing my playing. I was 'told' that it was Archangel Michael with his sword of truth to cut away bonds from the past that were limiting Victoria's forward progress of re-empowerment. Michael showed me an image of Victoria in a previous incarnation and she was like a warrior goddess, a very fierce, powerful being. She had chosen to come back in her present form to find humility and gentle strength, but unfortunately over time and through various situations and relationships, she had given all of her power away. She is a gentle soul and a pure heart and our animal guides, especially Freddy, who had been her dog and was now in spirit, wanted her to reclaim her power and use it in a gentle way this time. The healing from the bowl seemed to enable Victoria to see herself stripped of all limitation, as a beautiful light being. When my dog Winnie performed her final healing for Victoria at the end of the session, I asked what she was doing and she said she was confirming to Victoria that Freddy was orchestrating things and had been all along. The way Winnie lay across Victoria's lap was just how Freddy would have done it — Winnie is not prone to doing this normally but she always seems to know what is required in her healing sessions with 'our' clients. Once again I was amazed at the capacity of our animals to know exactly what we need to be healed. It was a reminder to me to appreciate all the help and guidance my own animals give, not only to me but also to the people who come to me for healing — they are indeed wonderful 'colleagues'.

Below is Victoria's account of her session.

My dog Rufus has issues with horses and cars, lunging and barking at them. He also dislikes being handled and I cannot put a harness on him. It turned out that Rufus had been a starving wolf in a past life; he was the pack's alpha male, I was the alpha female and we had cubs. In this life, Rufus had his back broken by a stallion while trying to feed the family by preying on a herd of horses. We decided to rewrite the scene by having him successfully and quickly kill a foal that was not as fit and well as the other horses. With the new 'script', Rufus made the kill and I felt his emotions; he was feeling confident, secure and successful. His back then needed healing, and although Madeleine offered to do this, Rufus wanted me to be the one to do it — he wanted me to prove to myself that I could do it. I visualized his spine, working my way down until I found a 'spongy' section that Madeleine confirmed as the part where the old fracture was still affecting him. I was then guided to laser some healing light from my index and middle finger into this area, and it soon became solid and matched the rest of his healthy spine. Rufus confirmed that he was now healed and the hair along his back, which had been standing up, was now lying flat. Polly told of her trauma in her current lifetime over being spayed, which is something that she had brought up in her reading with Madeleine when I first got her. She had been handed in to a pound in Ireland very heavily pregnant; she gave birth to stillborn puppies and was spayed soon afterwards, and was ill and depressed for about a month. At this stage I adopted her and Madeleine healed most of this trauma. However, two years on she still carries some physical trauma as she felt that it was very brutal. She also wanted to flag up a similar issue of mine—I have been sterilized, which I now regret, not because I have changed my mind about not wanting children but because I feel that I have mutilated my body. Also, I have been raped in the past.

I visualized the inside of Polly's body and saw a dark patch on the left side of her abdomen. Again using laser light from my first two fingers, I replaced the dark patch with healing light until I felt that she was healed. She then told me to do the same to myself, so I visualized the inside of my own body and found a dark patch in the same place as Polly's. I did the healing light exercise on myself and felt healed. I now feel much better and happier about being able to have a relationship.

Both of my dogs wanted me to be healed. They also wanted to confirm what I have been told by my guides—that I really am capable of listening and of healing, not only them but myself as well.

When Madeleine's dog Winnie lay across my lap I found it very healing and comforting, as my soulmate dog Freddy used to lie on me in exactly the same way. Winnie told Madeleine that I needed to check my emotional heart, which I did, and found some dark areas. I zapped them with my laser light and turned the dark areas very bright and light. Winnie was happy that I had done all I needed to that day.

This had been an incredible session, but we weren't finished yet—Victoria's dog Freddy came through again. As we will see, this story beautifully illustrates the subject of the next chapter.

CHAPTER 4

Can we release connected traumas?

The relationships we have with our animals are so very special. Once we find the reasons for our connections, so much becomes clear. I don't think that we ever 'get over' the loss of a loved one, but awareness of the bigger picture behind their passing can ease our pain and make it more manageable. Victoria's grief for Freddy had never subsided; the pain was still as raw even though years had passed.

Freddy — Victoria's Soulmate from Spirit

As we shall see, though, the pain was there so that Victoria could finally understand and move towards healing and resolution. Time, as the saying goes, is a great healer and it is important to try to reflect on the blessings, fun and unconditional love that our animal friends bring us, as that is their deepest wish and the reason why they find us and come to share and enrich our lives. It works the other way round, too; in our previous incarnations we humans will have played our part in enriching their lives.

I came to Madeleine for a healing treatment as I had some issues—I couldn't bear water on my face or hands, and I was unable to touch a dead animal—which I felt stemmed from a past life. I have also suffered from insomnia for the last seven years, which I was sure had started after a bout of flu. My soulmate dog Freddy passed to spirit three years ago and I am still struggling to deal with the grief and the physical loss of him. I also had sore feet and a sore left shoulder.

We worked through my chakras to see if a past-life memory was being held in them, and when we got to my sacral chakra I felt very tense and could see dead beech leaves. Madeleine could see me as Rebecca, a medieval white witch and herbalist, with very pure and high intentions. Rebecca had treated an animal, a stray dog, which had then been poisoned by someone in the village who was looking for an excuse to get rid of the 'witch'. When the dog died, Rebecca ran into the woods to hide to escape the pursuers who were shouting at her 'Meddling witch' and worse. She was barefoot and the soles of her feet were torn and bruised. Her shoulder also caught on a branch and wrenched. Eventually she was so exhausted she collapsed and covered herself in the beech leaves carpeting the ground. She struggled to stay awake so she could escape from her pursuers, but she finally succumbed to sleep and she was captured and dragged down to the stream by her hair with her hands clasped in front of her. As the villagers pushed Rebecca down to the stream they flung the dead dog at her while shouting and hurling insults. The dog, a mongrel, I recognized all of a sudden as the dog who was Freddy in this lifetime. His body was touching her shoulder as her head was pushed into the stream, her hands trapped underneath her body. Rebecca was drowned.

This explained such a lot. We were guided not to rewrite this past life yet, and indeed I felt that the rewrite should not come until we reached the heart chakra. I brought a white light down and changed the leaves to a springy carpet of grass, which was soft and held healing energy from the earth so that it not only protected but also actively helped my torn, sore feet. My feet felt much better and the pain in my shoulder also disappeared. The solar plexus chakra showed a very bright mustard-yellow light, too bright, which made me feel exposed and vulnerable—just as I had while I had relived my experience as Rebecca, fleeing through the woods. I brought a white light down and changed the light to a softer, safer feeling yellow. At my heart chakra, all I could see was a very dense black lump and a feeling of being frightened, lost, empty and despairing. We then rewrote the past life, and this time the remedy that Rebecca gave Freddy put him in a deep healing sleep—so deep that he seemed to be dead, so Rebecca still ran into the woods as before. This time, though, Freddy woke, healed. After a few days, the villagers searched for Rebecca to tell her that everything was OK, and the person who had been trying to find an excuse for removing the 'meddling witch' from the village was converted into seeing that, in fact, Rebecca was good. When they found her, this person carried her back to the village as atonement. Her feet were treated with healing balms and she was laid down on her bed, with Freddy curled up with her. She slept a deep, healing sleep, and woke up feeling safe, secure, and accepted as a valued member of the community. I could now see a pink centre in my heart chakra, with an emerald green surround.

Now when I think of Freddy I can smile and remember the joy we have had together rather than feeling torn apart because he isn't here. This has made such a change to my way of dealing with my life without Freddy. It always seemed strange to me that on the one hand I felt such terrible grief because he wasn't here physically, and yet on the other able to connect, exchange love with him and communicate intuitively with him so that I knew he was still with me. This experience explains it. He is my soulmate. I still miss his physical presence, but I have let go of the despair and pain and now feel more comfortably close to him, with a wonderfully secure and positive kind of love. My feet are better and the pain in my shoulder has gone. I can now tolerate water on my hands and face. I am processing the sleep issue and am confident that it will continue to improve.

I was thrilled with Victoria's progress and courage in facing this very traumatic experience. The relief in her face when we changed the outcome and the way she was perceived was tremendous; she seemed to grow in stature before my very eyes as she regained her self-esteem and self-confidence — thanks to Freddy.

Old Dogs Do Not Die

We have a secret, you and I,
That no one else shall know,
For who, but I can see you lie,
Each night, in fire glow?
And who but I can reach my hand
Before we go to bed,
And feel the living warmth of you
And touch your silken head?
And only I walk woodland paths,
And see, ahead of me,
Your small form racing with the wind,
So young again, and free.
And only I can see you swim
in every brook I pass.
And, when I call, no one but I
can see the bending grass.

The next case was my first experience of rewriting a past-life script and I am extremely grateful to Jess for teaching me how to facilitate these incredible healings with the help of the animals. Jess has been the catalyst for me to use this new technique in many healing sessions.

> *"The horse already understands the human better than the human will ever understand the horse."*
>
> D. BENNET

Jess — The Green-Eyed Mare

"My horse is so jealous!" Jenny complained over the phone. She had rung me because her new horse, Jess, seemed to object violently to any time Jenny spent with her other two horses, Tigger and especially her other mare, Vienna. If Jenny made a fuss of Vienna, or even just groomed her, Jess would get angry and start to kick and bang her stable door and lay her ears back. Jenny was concerned that Jess might injure herself, and as she didn't own the stable yard where she kept her horses, she was also worried that she would be asked to leave if Jess continued like this.

Although Jenny told me that she was spending the majority of her time schooling and exercising Jess, as Vienna and Tigger were no longer rideable, it seemed that this was still not enough; if Jenny even popped into Vienna's stable, Jess would lunge and try to bite Vienna over the stable door. When the horses were out in their field, however, Vienna was the dominant mare. Other users of the stables also told Jenny that the mares got on fine when she wasn't there.

I was looking forward to meeting Jess and hearing her side of what sounded like a very intriguing case. When I arrived at the stable yard, Vienna's lovely chestnut head was straining out over her door to see who had arrived—I recognized her as we had met before when I had been called out to ask her if she wanted to be ridden any more. Tigger was busy munching his hay, but Jess lunged up to the door with her eyes practically out on stalks, already in a state of anxiety as to who I was and what I was doing there. She was a beautiful piebald mare and I felt that she had huge potential to excel in her ridden career, in whatever way she most enjoyed. Jenny told me that when Jess was ridden, she was brilliant and generally quite well behaved, but that she seemed permanently anxious when out exercising and, particularly in confined narrow places, was on permanent tenterhooks. I had a feeling that this piece of information was very significant, but I started by gently probing Jess's thoughts with my mind, hoping to get a better understanding of where she was coming from emotionally. I felt a sense of frustration as Jess whirled around the stable in a flurry of concern, but she seemed unwilling to open up to me telepathically, so I patiently kept reassuring her and telling her that I was there to help, that she was safe and that I would do my utmost to resolve whatever was troubling her.

Eventually Jess told me that she always tried to please and to do her best, to which Jenny agreed. However, Jess was very upset that despite her best efforts in her last home, she had been the one to be sold on while other horses stayed. It was as though she thought I might be coming to take her away while Vienna and Tigger, who weren't even ridden any more, would be kept. Poor Jess was so frustrated and exasperated as to what more she could do to be valued and understood. Finally she began to show me a past life involving herself, Jenny, Tigger and Vienna. It was as though the Universe had contrived to bring them all together again, to finally resolve and heal a trauma that was still impacting on all of them.

With Jess's help I started to visualize a scene that appeared to be in North America, where Jenny, in this life a man, was riding Tigger and leading two packhorses –Vienna and Jess—through mountainous terrain. Jess, bringing up the rear, was attached to Vienna by a lead rope. As they were making their way through a very narrow passage between some rocks, a huge mountain lion suddenly dropped onto Jess's back, biting and breaking her neck, and poor Jess fell to the ground. Vienna and Tigger fled in terror as Jenny struggled to control them. She looked back and saw that it was futile trying to return to save Jess; she could see that the mare was dying, so she continued distancing herself from the horrific attack, hoping to at least save the other horses and herself. Jess's dying vision was of being left to die as the others fled to safety.

Before I recounted this vision, I asked Jenny how she felt, in this life, when she was riding through the narrow path that she had told me about. She had described a narrow path with a steep overhang, lined with trees, and said that when riding through there, she always felt as though something might drop down on them as if in ambush. She said she knew it sounded silly and she couldn't really explain it, but that she found it frightening. Thanks to Jess I was able to explain; as I described Jess's awful death I could feel a huge weight in my heart, and Jenny said that she felt enormous guilt, sadness and grief that she could not save Jess. We discussed other aspects of Jenny's life where she felt she had failed and let herself, and others, down. Jenny's life so far had not gone smoothly; I felt that there was an underlying issue of guilt wrapped up in a lack of self-worth, as though she was still punishing herself for not being able to save Jess in this past life. Here was a huge opportunity to heal that trauma for all concerned. I asked Jenny to imagine being back in that time, feeling the rope in her hand, feeling Tigger beneath her and seeing the rocky out-crop where the mountain lion had suddenly appeared. Jess facilitated the rewriting of their past-life 'video clip' by showing Jenny what she'd looked like as a man and what colour and type the horses had been in this incar-nation. Jenny was quite a grizzled old prospector, used to rough living and the chance to pan some gold from the unyielding terrain. Tigger looked more like a mule and Vienna and Jess were quite chunky, stolid little bays. Once Jenny could visualize and describe herself and the horses I knew we were all set to rewrite their story. I encouraged her, with the help of Jess, to change the outcome so that it didn't end so tragically. This time Jenny shot the mountain lion before it could attack, and they all rode away safe and sound. When Jenny had finished, it seemed as though a huge weight had lifted from her, and Jess also immediately looked calmer, her eyes, which had been so wild, softened. Her 'red alert' attitude had completely gone. I hoped that the impact of this would filter out into Jenny's life and once again marvelled at the extraordinary ways in which the Universe, together with the help of the animals, can orchestrate such fantastic reso-lution and healing.

A few days later, I was dining out with a friend at a local pub and happened to bump into the owner of the yard. She reported that Jess was a changed horse — very calm, not sulking or angry, getting on well with Vienna and Jenny. Jenny was pleased with her progress and was beginning to appreciate how Jess's changed behaviour was help-ing her move forwards in her own life.

CHAPTER 5

Will we meet again?
How will we know?

So many people want to know if their animals will come back to them. It's a question that I too want to know the answer to. People always ask how they will know and what will happen if they choose the wrong pet, and they want to know how they will recognize their old pets. I think it is worth saying again that there are no mistakes and no coincidences. Our animals find *us*. They are expert at orchestrating the next steps in our combined lives. It's lovely when a pet shows me what their future incarnation may look like, but they don't always do this as sometimes they don't wish to influence their owner's experience. However, in the following story you will see that a Rottweiler called Brandi showed me very clearly that she would be returning in the same guise.

Silvia and Brandi

Brandi's owner, Silvia Davalos, had lost three dogs in the preceding nine months. Ben (her "saint") was nine; his death was not unexpected due to his age, breed and size. Later, Summer, a Rottweiler only three years of age who had recently had puppies, suddenly passed. One of Summer's puppies, Brandi, then died at only seven and a half months old of peritonitis that was caught too late to save her.

She had had intestinal surgery and Silvia wondered if this could have been related to her death. She was finding Brandi's death extremely difficult to deal with and had a guilty conscience about it. Silvia needed to know why she was taken so young, and also wanted to tell her that she was sorry she had stayed with the vet, who admitted that he had neglected her and was insensitive to the situation.

Silvia felt that Summer called her daughter to be with her, as Brandi was her favourite and Summer had always taken time to play with her individually.

What sweethearts! I feel that Summer and Brandi were very connected and had a pre-agreed contract to stay for just a short while on this plane. I think that Brandi wanted to experience a short stay, just to try out her doggy physical body, but that she was never really grounded here. She had so much love though, from both her mother and her human 'mum'. And Summer stayed long enough to give birth to Brandi, which was their agreement and how they managed to orchestrate their incarnation and life purpose this time around. As far as the bigger picture goes, this situation is perfect, but of course on the human level you must be devastated and it must seem like such a waste for their lives to have been cut so short in such a tragic fashion.

If you have read my book , you will have read about my lovely dog Pillow, who died so young. I was absolutely heartbroken, but she has come back to me from spirit to explain, and also sent Winnie, our brindle rescue dog, who you can see on my website. Winnie was picked up by the dog warden almost to the second that Pillow was killed, as we were told by a friend of ours who witnessed it. I believe Pillow orchestrated the whole thing—she told me that she found being in a physical body just too heavy and that she wanted to be pure energy. I feel Brandi will come back and I think Summer will stay longer to be her protector in spirit. If you're planning on breeding more dogs, she may well be one of the pups in the litter, or if you don't breed any more yourself, you will get a message about a puppy and one look and you'll know that it's her. I know how much of a shock it is when they pass, especially in this case when they were both so young. But try to be comforted that they are fine, planning and plotting their return! As her mother Summer said, she will be waiting in spirit and I wouldn't be surprised if she comes back as Brandi's baby next time round. I feel that this is a role they've taken turns with over many lifetimes. I'm sure you've had other lifetimes with them too, maybe being pups in the same litter (no wonder you love dogs so much!!).You are very loved by all your dogs, both in the physical world and in spirit, so have no fear; both Brandi and Summer will find their way back to you. I feel that they will be Rotties, but be open to whatever unfolds—you may be surprised. Brandi really wants to get back to you to reassure you. I'm feeling that Brandi was not cleaned properly when they made the incision into the peritoneum and that the vet was in a rush. I think the incision got infected, which she managed to fight to a certain extent, but her immune system could not fight both this and the infection, as she was weakened and depleted from her operation.

This love will never die; you will all keep going round in your various guises until you have learnt what needs to be learnt. Let me know when she arrives!

There are several homoeopathic remedies that might be very beneficial with helping you with your grief—not to forget, just to manage it a little better. I know only too well how awful it is. Perhaps try Nat Mur.

Brandi returns

Silvia contacted me about a year later with an update: she had decided not to breed dogs again in the near future, but for some reason she could not fully explain she had made contact with another Rottweiler breeder who was expecting a litter. Silvia had a very good feeling about this but wanted to hear from me whether it would be possible that Brandi would be in this new litter and would come back. She said that Brandi's sister, Gretchen, missed Brandi as much as she herself did. She asked if there was anything she could do to help Brandi come back. I felt that the Universe, with Brandi's help, was contriving to send her back to Silvia; I am a great believer in listening to your inner voice and I feel that there is no such thing as coincidence. I suggested that Silvia sit quietly with a picture of Brandi and maybe a collar of hers and get a sense and a mental image of her eyes, as that would be the best way to recognize her in the new litter. I also suggested that she try sitting in a spot that was Brandi's favourite and allowing Brandi's energy to fill her body. This can be emotional but I counselled Silvia to just let the tears flow if they wanted to as they would be tears of joy.

Silvia's final update speaks for itself. Here it is, in her own words.

> Hi Madeleine,
>
> On Wednesday 29 June my friend and I went to pick up our puppies. Out of the two, one with a purple collar and one with a black collar, the purple was very friendly and not shy but the black-collar one liked being independent and it took her a while to approach me.
>
> The breeder wanted me to take the purple-collared one as she was top show quality and had a more correct structure for her breed. I felt more drawn to the puppy with the black collar though.
>
> When my friend and I took our puppies back to the hotel things began to change. My puppy began to show dominance and when we took them out on walks she tried to eat everything she found on the ground –bugs, rocks—just like my 'first' Brandi. When I brought her home it was as if she knew the house—she seemed to feel right at home straight away. She even knew her name within hours of being here and has become an escape artist, just like Brandi.
>
> Gretchen, within two days of Brandi being in the house, has acquired a new best friend. They play together and I know I could trust them alone together.
>
> As soon as I take good pictures of Brandi I will send them.
>
> Thanks for all the advice that you've given me.
>
> Silvia

Tessie and Bailey

I love to hear that our pets come back –it's so wonderful to know that we never really lose them. Another lovely story along the same lines is from Josie, who had contacted me because she was devastated by her lovely dog Tessie's passing. Her other dog Roly was also pining for Tessie's physical presence. Here is the exchange we had:

Maternal love and loyalty.

These are the words that underpin the whole reading. As I gaze into Tessie's eyes, I see such devotion and it's easy to see the deep bond between you all. I feel she has a very nurturing nature and will still be using those skills while she is in spirit. I think her old body just let her down eventually and she has needed to pass in order to become rejuvenated and find a new physical vehicle to continue her precious work. She is a very special being and was always wise beyond her years. She has taught you all so much and Roly will be missing her guidance. She had a very 'mother hen' sort of energy and I feel that she was always there with soft cuddles and wet nose to comfort you if you'd had a bad day or were feeling down about anything. She seems to have taken on a huge role in this previous life and I feel she will be coming back for some playtime. Maybe Roly will come into her own now as she will need to find a way to blossom instead of having Tessie to rely on. I feel that Tessie's internal organs didn't function so well in the end and that she was worn out from carrying so much responsibility. Please don't get upset by this, though; it was her chosen role and she loved it. She's showing me a very lively cream-coloured puppy with quite pale eyes but a huge depth to them. I think you'll have your hands full! Tessie is showing me a blonde lady wearing a yellow top and gold jewellery, very big hearted; she is either the breeder or the person who will, in whatever way, put you in touch with the litter where you will find Tessie again.

Roly has been feeling quite lost, and will feel a very big gap or void in the household, as I'm sure you feel too. I think you both miss her so much because she was such a protective loving force in your home. The Bach flower remedy Star of Bethlehem may work well for both you and Roly, and the homoeopathic remedy Ignatia could also be very helpful in getting you through this very tough time.

I feel that Tessie came into your life to teach you about love and being able to trust in opening your heart to love and trust. I feel you have had some very hard times, when your trust in others has been lost and you have felt disinclined to open your heart, Tessie says that you have learned well and that just because you are feeling such strong feelings of grief and loss, you shouldn't shut your heart down again; instead you should try to let go of the pain and embrace the love that you shared and will share again in the future. Unfortunately, calculating 'time' in spirit is very difficult as time is very different there, but hang on in there, be open to the surprises she has in store for you and hang onto your hat for when this new puppy enters your house like a whirlwind!

Josie's response is very heart-warming.

Just letting you know we have a new puppy who we have named Bailey. He is cream with white markings and I came across him on the internet and couldn't take my eyes off his eyes. It was like his eyes were pulling me in; I know it sounds strange, but when I look at him now I still feel that pulling feeling, as though I can't take my eyes off his When I first got him I was happy, sad ... I had very mixed emotions for a while, and was feeling guilty because of Tessie. Roly seems to get upset with him a lot but hope-fully it will calm down.

You were right—Bailey is a whirlwind. And you were also right about the lady with blonde hair—she is the breeder. You were right again when you said Tessie had a lot of surprises in store for us!

As I mentioned earlier, timescales can be difficult to predict, but sometimes things do not take long at all to happen. I did a reading for someone who had lost a cat called Smokey, in which I was shown a black kitten that I was led to understand would reveal itself to Smokey's grieving owner when the time was right. I wasn't expecting to hear back from her quite as soon as I did, but her response arrived by return:

I can't believe it, Madeleine! I just finished reading your lovely messages, when I noticed something at the window out of the corner of my eye and there was a little black face with the most enormous yellow eyes, staring in at me. It was a black kitten! I opened the window and it just strolled in like it owned the place. I just know Smokey sent her to me.

She updated me again later by saying that she had tried to find the kitten's owner, but no one in the area had reported a black kitten missing and she drew a blank. How wonderful that Smokey found a way back, and how amazing that he arrived so quickly after giving me the message and his description of his new incarnation.

"Knowledge speaks but wisdom listens"
JIMI HENDRIX

Noon, the Catalyst

The following is an amazing account of a person, whose harrowing trauma had stayed with her for over fifty years, and of her journey towards healing and closure. This healing journey was all thanks to a cat named Noon, horses Micah, Crystal, Pashar and Merlin and a steer named Tesoro!

Gillian was a very accomplished lady, a holistic practitioner who was very knowledgeable about all sorts of healing modalities. However, for most of her life she had been plagued by the most awful childhood memory. She had kept it bottled up for many years, along with the distressing emotions that came with it, but it would keep rearing its ugly head.

Noon, the CATalyst

When Gillian arrived at a retreat that I was co-facilitating at a ranch in Canada, she was in quite a stressed state. I suspect that she wondered what she'd let herself in for, but she gamely joined in with all the activities. She worked well with the horses, learning natural horsemanship and connecting with members of the herd who chose to interact with us as equine 'therapists'. She also discussed her husband and how, although he loved his horses, he was traditional in his approach. She had doubts about whether she would be able to convert him to this new free, gentle way of working with horses. He sounded like a lovely man but not someone who was prone to any rash or spontaneous acts — or so we thought!

On the second day, Gillian was lying on one of the healing tables that had been set up in a way that the horses could choose to come over and interact. The animal who started the proceedings on this day, though, was not a horse but a beautiful black lion of a cat whose name was Noon. He seemed very keen to make his presence felt, which was interesting, as Gillian had mentioned that ever since her childhood trauma, she had felt that she would never be able to own a cat. She thought she would never be able to keep a cat safe, a feeling that stemmed from the childhood event and her helplessness in it. I interpreted Noon's healing messages and one of the young horses, Micah, came over to reassure Gillian and add her own healing energy. While I was working, Noon announced, clear as day, in my head: 'I'm the catalyst! She needs to get some cats back in her life.'

Tesoro

He seemed very proud of himself for making such a play on words. I'll let you read Gillian's story so that you can draw your own conclusions, but I feel that those kittens returned in exactly the same number, to bring a final close to Gillian's lifelong pain and all instigated by the 'catalyst', Noon!

The first time I lay on the table, the 'black magic' cat, Noon, jumped up, seemingly agitated, and ran back and forth from between my shoulder and my feet. The next morning, I felt very emotional and that old incident with my father and the kittens was again nagging at me. I had worked on this using many different modalities, but although my work would chip away at another level and move me towards releasing it fully, it was still always there.

Through all the love and healing of that week, and the special attention I've received from Micah, Crystal, Merlin and Paschar and, most distinctly, Tesoro, I believe that I have finally let it go. I remember one moment when Tesoro's head appeared beside me and I saw a tear roll down his big cow face. I was surprised but also so moved at this visible confirmation; it was as though he had taken on all of the difficulties for me.

At home after the retreat, I was with my husband Don and my five-year-old grandson Kevin, when Don said Kevin had something to show me outside. We went down to the barn together and there were not one, but five rescued kittens: three black females, a white male with black markings and a white male with grey markings. For just a brief moment I had a flashback to long ago, of five kittens wearing dolls' hats and clothes. This vision would normally bring with it strong feelings of fear, and tears, but this time the picture disappeared almost immediately and as I played with the kittens I cried no tears and felt no despair—only love.

Let me explain. I was four years old, playing on my own as my other siblings were at school or indoors. I was sitting on the end of the sidewalk in front of our house with five kittens in a box, with my dolls' clothes and blankets and hats, and was dressing the kittens. My doll buggy was waiting and I was going to take them for a walk.

My father, on his way out to the barn, stopped close to me. I sat very still, feeling—knowing—that something bad was going to happen. He reached down and took a kitten and I watched him walk away, wondering where he was taking it. He stopped about five feet away from me, by a telephone pole, and whacked the kitten's head on the pole, then came back and dropped it into the box. He took another one; this time I didn't watch, but when I looked down at the box the kitten had an eye hanging out of the socket and blood coming from its mouth. From then on I just stared straight ahead.

When he had finished with all five, he said, "The farm has too many cats—we can't keep them all. Go and put them on the manure pile." I did as I was told, and dumped them, just like garbage. One was still twitching but I didn't know what to do and knew I couldn't save it from my father anyway. I dumped my dolls' clothes and blankets too.

For some time after that, I believed that my father could kill me too and I was very afraid of him. I saw him abuse other animals—he would kick a cow if it didn't move fast enough or spilled a milk bucket. I don't think he imagined, or could have understood, how much he had damaged me. I have never been able to come to terms with how or why he did that in front of me.

I never told anyone about it. I buried it, and only started to deal with it at all at the age of almost fifty when I began to work on my personal issues on courses like Madeleine's.

Only God knows why there is such inhumanity to man and beast on this planet, and it still boggles my mind, but now for the first time in my life, I know I have found peace on this issue. I have been able to type this story for the first time and there are no tears or heaviness, just a little sadness that it even occurred, but mainly a feeling of freedom.

CHAPTER 6

Can health issues be healed by past-life therapy?

I am consistently and regularly amazed at the—sometimes instant—physical results that can occur if people can heal the past. It's as though by discovering the origin of the physical symptom and releasing the fear and trauma connected to it, the body no longer needs to carry that trauma at a cellular level. I am constantly in awe of the power of our minds; we have barely scratched the surface when it comes to understanding what we are truly capable of. It makes perfect sense to me that if we can create imbalance in our bodies through our thoughts, then we can also reverse these symptoms by the same process—by using our inner knowing and positive self-belief. However, it does seem to be a human trait to allow fear and negativity to reign within us rather than to focus on positive, fearless love. Focusing on love is harder, and can take a lot of effort to achieve, but I believe that being mindful of our inner conversations can really help. Traumas can be stored so deep within us that it can be difficult to access the negative memories in order to clear them; luckily, though, our animals can show us the way. In the following case, I describe what was the most dramatic 'shift' that I have yet witnessed.

Seamus, Mary and Raj

I was called out to a livery yard to meet a lovely horse called Seamus, a beautiful dappled grey. He stomped nervously, snorting through his flared nostrils, as I gently tried to reassure him that I was there to help. He had some fears about being loaded into a horsebox and also had confidence issues with being ridden. I discovered, though, that as well as these immediate and very real issues, there was a deeper reason for his behaviour. His deeper worry was to do with a horse who he thought badly needed my help. Seamus' owner thought he might be referring to her daughter's horse, Raj, who she thought was becoming increasingly unpredictable, to the point where she sometimes worried for the safety of her daughter, Mary. Seamus showed me Raj by, I swear, *winking* at me and pointing with his head in the direction of a large chestnut horse at the end of the barn. I heard him say in my head, clear as day, 'For goodness sake, sort them out! They've got *real* issues'. Raj eyed me a little suspiciously as I neared his box. He was a very large and powerful horse and Mary looked rather diminutive next to him. Mary described some of the problems she had been having with Raj, namely how he had lost his confidence and that he seemed to have a real issue with turning to the left. When I questioned Raj, my mind connecting telepathically with his, he said that he needed Mary to be more confident in herself so that she could be a stronger leader for him. If she believed in him, he could then believe in himself. I noticed a large splash of much darker fur on his right shoulder, surrounded by a white outline. Mary said that she had been told that he was born with this mark and that as far as she was aware there had been no injury to his shoulder. However, there were bells going off in my head, so I tuned in to the energy of the shoulder. I asked Raj to show me what was going on and if this was the cause of his concerns. I could 'see' pieces of shrapnel-like metal, existing only as an energy but embedded as a memory within Raj's shoulder. My actions as I visualized removing these energetic pieces of metal must have looked rather strange, and I'm sure Mary and her mother wondered what on earth I was doing as I physically plucked what looked to them like thin air out of Raj's shoulder! When I'd finished I visualized filling the area with healing light, at which point Mary started to feel a stabbing pain in her own left shoulder. I described the 'clip' that Raj was running through my mind. I was being shown a past life in a Napoleonic battle. I could see Raj as a powerful grey horse and Mary as a male soldier, charging through a battlefield in the midst of cannon fire. Mary and Raj were hit broadside as a cannon exploded next to them, and flung metal into Raj's shoulder, throwing them sideways onto their left side. Sadly, Raj's wounds were too serious for him to survive, but although Mary was crushed beneath the dying horse she did somehow survive. She sustained severe injuries, though, that left her with a withered arm and a much-weakened left side.

I worked to remove the negative memory from Mary's arm, and asked her if she could imagine the scene that Raj had shown me. To her amazement she was able to describe every detail of her uniform and how they had both looked in that lifetime. Mary could feel tingling as though something was changing in her arm. She then told me that she had always been very weak in her left arm and, in fact, in her whole left side, and that she had found it difficult to steer and control Raj because of this weakness. I felt sure that this had a lot to do with his difficulty in turning to the left. The renewed energy in Mary's arm was a little blocked at the elbow, so I asked Raj to help me to clear it. He guided me to ask Mary to visualize little taps at the ends of her fingers, so that we could open them and allow the blocked energy to be released. I pretended to turn the imaginary taps, visualizing dark treacly energy coming out, and asked Mary what she would like to transmute it into. Mary said she could imagine daisies floating skyward and taking the entire trauma away. She also visualized the pain in her shoulder being carried away on daisies, and released a block in her head by blowing daisies out of her mouth. I thought this was particularly interesting as one homoeopathic remedy for deep-tissue trauma is Bellis Perennis, which comes from the daisy plant. I then asked Mary to visualize changing the outcome of the battle so that she and Raj could dodge the cannon fire and gallop to safety. Suddenly, Mary went white as a sheet and exclaimed that she felt very sick. She looked as though she was about to pass out, so I suggested that she sit down. She slid down the stable wall and sat in a heap looking alarmingly pale. Raj then gave a huge sigh and almost collapsed onto the straw, his eyes tightly closed and his muzzle pressed against the floor as he snorted and groaned. I was rather alarmed—I had never seen quite such a dramatic response from either animal or owner before. However, I knew that it was down to a huge energetic shift in their bodies' cellular memories, so I guided Mary to take some deep breaths and to allow herself to rest. While she did so, we visualized new energy filling her left arm, and when it reached her fingertips we imagined turning off the taps to seal in all this new healing energy. Eventually, the colour started to return to Mary's cheeks and she felt strong enough to stand, although Raj was still out for the count and breathing heavily. He had worked so hard to help Mary and himself release the past that he needed to rest for a while, recover and adjust to his new energy. As Mary's mother and I helped her into the house for a cup of tea, Mary almost screamed that her whole left side felt different and much stronger. When she was handed a mug of tea she was amazed to find that she could squeeze her mug, whereas before she had never been able to make a strong fist with her left hand. On our way back to check on Raj, as we passed Seamus he said, in my head,

'Thank goodness, about time!' When we reached the barn there was Raj, nonchalantly leaning over his stable door, cool as a cucumber and looking as though nothing had happened. His eyes were calm and, in contrast to his previous demeanour, he seemed very happy and relaxed.

After advising Mary to rest both herself and Raj as much as possible over the next couple of days, I left, reflecting on the chain of events that had led me to them and wondering whether Seamus in his wisdom had exaggerated his behaviour to force his owner to call me out and 'discover' the bigger issue of Mary and Raj and their problems. The visible physical effects on Mary and Raj of investigating their past life and releasing its traumas had been astonishing. I had been forced to really listen to my guidance and trust that even though their response had been so dramatic, it had been essential so that the deepest possible healing could occur.

Lady — The "Upside Down" Horse

Many cases involve not only much physical challenge but also emotional ones; in fact the two are often inextricably linked. Physical problems triggered by memories from a past life are very often just one part of a complex web of issues that needs to be untangled. In the following case, inexplicable fear and pain surfaced in both horse and rider, with perfect timing for the optimum healing to take place on all levels.

Christina was woken by a stabbing, searing pain in her leg. Even though she had just been asleep in bed all night, her leg was so painful that she felt as if she had broken it; in fact, as she shouted in terror for her mother, the words she used were, "Mum, I think I've broken my leg!" With help, Christina got out of bed and after a little while her leg started to function more normally. She was still in pain, but she and her mother decided that she would soldier on—they had animals to feed and care for.

The family had numerous animals in their care, but the one that was causing the most concern was Lady, a beautiful dun pony. She was now eighteen years old and they had owned her for six years. Over the last few years her desire and ability to jump had been deteriorating, with no reason that they could see. Today, the day of Christina's 'phantom' leg break, they had arranged for me to come and try to get to the bottom of what was affecting Lady so badly.

Brian, a black corgi cross who looked about half the height and twice the length of most dogs, greeted me and carefully monitored the proceedings. He ushered me to Lady's stable, where her lovely dun face was watching my approach with anticipation. I was equally keen to meet Lady as I had in advance examined a hair sample from her tail and studied her photograph, both of which had given me some very interesting details.

I wasn't aware of Christina's problem until she staggered slightly and her mother asked if she would rather sit down to rest her leg. They then explained that morning's strange events. I knew instinctively that this issue was connected with Lady and her fear; from examining Lady's hair sample and photograph, I'd been able to visualize a horrific break in the pony's back, which showed up like a shadowy line across the photograph. Holding the hair from her tail had given me a powerful feeling of terror. As Lady's soft sad eyes shone out at me, she telepathically asked me to question Christina as to her impressions and emotions when they'd first met. Christina told me that when she went to view Lady she had felt that the pony looked very sad, and that she was very thin and her current living environment was not ideal. Even more strange and interesting, though, she went on to say that she had felt that Lady was 'upside down', as though her neck and back bent in the wrong direction. Christina also said that she had simultaneously felt a deep sadness within her and a deep conviction that she and Lady just had to be together, without quite understanding why.

At Lady's then home, Christina and her mother were told of Lady's jumping prowess and shown her many rosettes from her glorious wins, so they were very puzzled when, after a few months at her new home, she still seemed to be so fearful. She'd never had any bad experiences and her saddle had been corrected and fitted perfectly. Her back had been treated by a professional equine therapist. She was competently ridden by Christina, a very accomplished rider, so why was the mare finding jumping so increasingly terrifying?

As I worked to send healing energy along Lady's back, I felt a block in the flow halfway along her back, between withers and pelvis. I could feel a 'break', a tissue memory from a past-life trauma, and a blue outline around Lady's body with a definite gap in it that showed me where the trauma had occurred. It was situated in the area of her solar-plexus chakra, which as we have seen earlier is an area where problems can affect self-worth and confidence on an emotional level. I then asked Lady to show me telepathically what had happened, and she asked me to find out which of Christina's legs was causing pain. When Christina told me it was her left leg, the significance hit me like a bolt of lightning. Of course! The two of them had been in whatever this incident was together, and they both had to resolve it here and now in order to progress with their lives. The left side of the body is thought of in many healing modalities and traditions as the female side, and most physical complaints to that side are believed to relate to female issues or people who have affected us emotionally. Leg conditions are usually thought of as indicating an inability to 'take the next step'. I felt that the female connection not only related to Lady being a mare but also to issues in Christina's life that were hindering her ability to move forward—something or someone was undermining her confidence and self-worth. This was connected, I felt sure, with the tangled past-life web that was beginning to unravel before me. As Lady relived her emotions I began to sense great fear. I could 'see' the pair of them galloping wildly across rocky terrain, desperately trying to escape from what looked like Mongolian marauders. They'd already galloped for miles over the open steppes when I saw that they were rushing headlong towards a deep rocky ravine that would prevent their safe passage as they tried to flee from their attackers. Christina in this life was a young man, dressed in leather and fur, and Lady was a very dark, chunkier-looking beast with a multi-coloured saddle blanket and a simple saddle and bridle. There was no other means of escape, so Lady courageously leapt into the ravine but fell and broke her back. The man who was Christina broke his left leg but was rescued by tribe members who had come to search for them. Sadly, Lady perished but Christina survived. She felt deep sadness at the loss of the faithful steed who had given her life to save her rider. As I was describing these scenes, I looked up and noticed that Christina was very pale and was shivering. I asked her if she had issues in her life that she was struggling to move on from, and if she felt undermined and undeserving of the best from life, and both she and her mother burst into tears. Christina said that she had been feeling very blocked and emotionally traumatized after some very upsetting relationship break-ups, which had left her very confused and stuck. Lady's problems about jumping were just making everything feel worse, as flying through the air on the back of her beautiful pony sometimes seemed to be the one pleasure that made Christina's life better. I asked her how the pain in her leg was, and she said that although it had felt momentarily worse it was now easing. I decided to ask Christina to rewrite their script so that this time both she and Lady survived. Once Christina could visualize the scene, she described Lady pecking slightly on landing but then recovering and galloping to safety among the other tribespeople. When she'd concluded, I asked her how she felt, and she said she was happy and the pain in her leg had miraculously disappeared. I then performed what I call 'soul retrieval' for Lady. I visualized her in her past incarnation healed and whole. Then I visualized 'blowing' that wholeness back into her, in order to replace a missing piece of soul that had been fragmented by the trauma of that terrible death. Both Lady and Christina now looked visibly brighter and we all had big grins on our faces. Lastly I performed some healing on Lady's back and visualized 'redrawing' her blue line so that her energetic blueprint was whole once more.

In a follow-on session with Christina, I helped her to let go of residual grief and guilt from this past life, so that she could know that she deserved the very best that life had to offer. Christina also came to understand that she was worthy of meeting the right person, who would recognize her strengths and both her inner and outer beauty. We realized that Lady had been destined to return to Christina so that they could both be healed. Lady's challenging and difficult behaviour with regard to jumping was now easier to understand; being with Christina had triggered her past-life fears of falling and sustaining a mortal injury. By discovering their shared past trauma and healing it, Christina was now able to let go of her deep-rooted sadness and guilt, thereby allowing both of them to move on and fear-lessly embrace life. We also marvelled at the synchronicity of Christina's 'broken leg' happening on the morning of my visit so that the issue could be addressed—all thanks to Lady!

Fiona and Belle

This next case, related by the animal's owner, illustrates a fascinating experience, where the owner not only visualized and witnessed a pet's past life but also witnessed her own pet 'speaking' to another animal in that past life in order to resolve and heal the issues from it.

Belle has a condition called syringomyelia, a painful condition affecting the neck. It had got to the point where, while out on a walk, she was stopping every few minutes to scratch at the painful spot. She also regularly suffered from nightmares. Medication had not helped, so I contacted Madeleine.

At Madeleine's, she and I both 'tuned in' and connected to the afflicted area of Belle's neck, and I was immediately taken into a past life where I felt very sick. Madeleine could see an infected open wound.

I then saw that in this life, Belle had been a gazelle. She was in a small clearing in a forest and, horrifically, she was attacked by a lion, which threw her up into the air by her back legs and broke her neck. Madeleine explained to me how to 'rewrite the script' to change the outcome of the scene, so this time I imagined the moment before impact as a freeze-frame, in which Belle, in a very superior voice, spoke to the lion and told him that did he not know that the law of nature was to respect all life and that one must ask permission to take the life of another.

The lion, very humble, lowered his head in shame and said that he did know the law. He apologized and explained that he wanted Belle's pure energy to carry on into the lion species through his cubs.

Belle's Heart

Belle accepted his apology and told him that he may take her. When I 'returned' from witnessing Belle's past life, Madeleine and I together visualized mending the broken bones in her neck, then stitching the nerves, tissues, flesh and skin together. Madeleine finished by placing an imaginary crystal plate in Belle's neck. Madeleine had previously described to me that she used these etheric quartz-like crystals in many forms to facilitate healing within people and animals. We noticed how the lovely heart-shaped marks on Belle's cheeks seemed to have expanded until they looked almost as though they were in 3D. I had always thought that these marks epitomized her loving nature, and this seemed to prove it.

After the session, on the car journey home, Belle was very calm. Ever since then she has only scratched her neck occasionally, and she rarely has nightmares any more.

Anna and Magoo

The following case illustrates the power of visualization techniques, and tuning in to the guidance our animals bring us, to create the best healing result. I have found the 'Hall of Mirrors' technique discussed here a wonderful method of allowing people to witness the progression of their healing, which can be incredibly empowering.

Magoo was a large bay dressage horse with immense presence. When I first met him he had been a rather nervous youngster and we had successfully worked through a past-life trauma. The second time I saw him he was a much more mature and worldly-wise chap and much more self-assured; in fact he seemed to 'have his hoof on' the pulse and gave me the lowdown on all the comings and goings in his yard! One thing he told me was about how Anna's family's recently deceased collie used to scratch on a door when she was alive, and that she was still making her presence felt now. The whole family was devastated by her loss—Magoo told me that Anna's father, a farmer, pretended to be tough and unattached, but that he would secretly take himself into Magoo's barn and allow himself to express his grief for the collie who had been such an important part of the farm and the family's life. Anna confirmed that the old collie bitch did have a special way of scratching on the kitchen door and that she suspected her father was far more upset than he ever let himself show. Magoo even talked about the local equine dentist, who he said needed to come and give him a routine check-up but who was on holiday in France. How a horse would know this I rationally do not know, but Anna said she'd let me know, and a couple of weeks later rang me to say that the dentist had indeed been away in France. We were all amazed—especially the equine dentist, who resolved from then on to watch his Ps and Qs where Magoo was concerned in case he divulged anything sensitive to the whole yard!

Having worked with Anna before, I was struck by her intuitive abilities; she was a fledgling animal communicator and an extremely accomplished horsewoman. Unfortunately, she did not always recognize her skills and suffered from limiting self-doubt. She had bought another horse, Evie, and told me that she had felt compelled to buy her—their connection was so strong that the minute Anna sat on the lovely horse, she burst into tears. I intuited that they had been together before in a past life, not exactly in the Spanish Riding School in Vienna or the Cadre Noir in France, but certainly an equitation centre of excellence. From this past life it appeared that Anna had these great abilities within her and already 'knew' all she needed to be a top-class rider; she just needed to remember and apply her dormant skills. Luckily Evie had no such doubts!

On my next visit to the farm, all of the collies good-naturedly woofed and bounded around me, apart from Lottie. Anna had asked me to have a chat with this older bitch, as she felt that Lottie had deteriorated after the demise of the dog who had recently died. I felt that Lottie wasn't in any pain but just needed to come to terms with the fact that she could no longer charge around as she used to, having had a series of small strokes. In my session with Anna I was to help her with her confidence levels. I noticed that she had a splint on her left hand and she told me that she had strained her thumb. We did some warm-up breathing exercises where I ask my clients to breathe in a wonderful essence I use infused with quartz crystal energy. I then asked her to 'send' the essence to all the areas of her body where she felt she needed its calming, empowering effects. Anna reported that she could not feel her left arm at all—it seemed to be a completely empty space. She tried visualizing a beautiful purple colour coursing around her body, but nothing would enter the 'space' that was her left arm. As we saw from the previous case study, the left side of the body is thought of as the female side and I thought it was quite significant that Anna, who worked very hard manually on the farm, might be struggling with appreciating her femininity. I felt that through trauma she may have become fragmented, and that energetically speaking she had become 'detached' from her left arm. I asked her to use the technique that I call going into the 'Hall of Mirrors', a very useful technique that I use frequently to intuit the emotional and physical condition of a client. I also encourage clients to visualize their own images, which gives enormous insight as to what is going on for them symbolically on many levels. Firstly, I invited into my mind an image that represented Anna at that moment in time and was shown a roll of wonderful new turf, very green but as yet not quite embedded and settled into a lawn. In her book *Life Choices, Life Changes*, Dina Glouberman describes these techniques, which harness the power of symbolism and imagery. When Anna used the technique, she saw herself in the first mirror as a tiny version of herself, with her arm hardly distinguishable. Then, as if by magic, Magoo and Lottie appeared on the scene and I asked Anna to ask them for advice on how she could feel stronger and believe in herself more. Magoo said that all she had to do was believe, and that he would help her, as she had helped him believe in himself and become the wonderfully wise horse he was now. I asked Anna to look into another mirror, and she was amazed to find that she had grown tall and that her left arm was back in place. Magoo had sent his healing breath to strengthen the whole limb and it was now a vibrant, strong part of Anna's body once more. When Anna gazed into the next mirror she saw her current physical form overlaid with that of a beautiful Native American woman. This gave Anna a huge sense of empowerment and we felt that it indicated another past life, which no doubt held yet more skills for her to access. When looking into the final mirror Anna became quite emotional, as she was joined in it by many animals past and present from her current life, all thanking her and reiterating how skilled she was and how proud they were to have shared their lives with her. Lottie and Magoo were saying, "Just get on with it! You can do it!" Anna realized that if she found it too hard to feel strong for herself, she could do it for her animals, who she realized were supporting her all the way on her journey of self-discovery. When Anna visualized leaving the hall of mirrors, I asked her if there was anywhere else that she wanted to visit on this occasion in order to learn what she needed to progress further. I asked her to look out for another room where she might be able to glean more information, and she visualized finding a door with the words *SELF-DOUBT* written on it. I wasn't completely comfortable with this, as I think it is more effective to concentrate on positive messages. I was guided instead to suggest to Anna an ingenious and inspired exercise; I was to ask her to imagine the letters as coloured magnetic letters like the ones available to play with on fridges. I asked Anna to remove the word *DOUBT* and replace it with the new coloured magnetic letters to spell the word *BELIEF*, which she performed effortlessly. I asked her what had become of the old letters that she had visualized, and she said that Magoo had trampled and crushed them—he would clearly not allow her to doubt herself any more. I suggested that if she was troubled by any nagging thoughts in the future, she could literally rewrite her script in techno magnetic colour and ask Magoo to destroy the evidence again.

When Anna returned from her meditative state she looked completely different, revitalized and glowing. She said her arm felt strong, and she was amazed at the depth of devotion her animals had shown her and how much they had helped her. I reminded her that they were just repaying her kindness to them. She also felt stronger about the loss of her beloved horses and dogs, and reassured that when the time came for the old collie Lottie to pass, she would still be 'there' in spirit to guide her. Once again I marvelled at the commitment from our animal friends to guide and help us on our journey of empowerment.

CHAPTER 7

How can I learn to intuit my pet's past life?

I found the following case mind-blowing; if I was ever in any doubt about how deep our connections go with our animal companions, I need no further proof! Below, Sera tells the story of her experiences with her horse, Moon, in her own words. The regression in this case was one of the most extraordinary experiences I have ever been privileged to witness. One of the things this case taught me was that you should always trust your instincts, as Sera did here. If you feel a completely irrational desire to be with your potential puppy, kitten horse or whatever your new pet might be, *listen* to that desire and trust it. Often it is something in the eyes that triggers that feeling—a kind of deep knowing of each other on the soul level. Many clients have said to me that it was because of their eyes that they knew their previous pet had returned to them. I was moved to tears when I first met Sera and 'read' the photo of Moon that she gave me.

Sera and Moon—Past Life Connections

When I first met Moon, I was 21 and a tearaway. I went clubbing seven nights a week, sometimes getting home an hour before I had to go to work. The mare I had at the time died peacefully in her sleep after being retired for several years, and it brought home that I wanted to ride again, so I started to spend more time at the stables helping out and riding a horse for a friend. One day I went to another yard with a friend, purely to keep her company and for the trip, as I wasn't in a financial position to buy another horse and mentally I was not in a good place, so I definitely wasn't looking for a horse for myself. As we stood in the yard, the most beautiful horse I have ever seen was brought in from the field. I can't even begin to describe how much I wanted to have this horse in my life. I had never experienced such a strong feeling before and I had known and ridden hundreds of horses. She was 15.3hh, nine years old, a pure thoroughbred and mahogany bay with a star on her forehead, and I fell in love instantly. But I was two weeks too late. Moon belonged to South West Equine Protection (SWEP) and the lady who had her on loan was rehoming her. A new home had been found for Moon, but she was lame in her shoulder so wasn't yet able to move. Moon had been rescued by SWEP in a terrible state, with abscesses in all four hooves, very thin and with a pelvis injury. Despite it all she was a very sweet-natured horse. Moon was nearly put to sleep at the end of 2003 as she had had ten bad attacks of colic in the space of eight weeks, but when the time came, she stole a carrot from her interim owner's pocket and the owner could not bring herself to send Moon off.

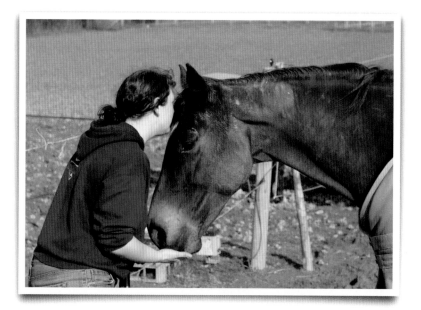

Moon and Sera

Two weeks after my first sighting of Moon, I still couldn't get her out of my head. I had been offered several other horses to try out on loan, but I couldn't bring myself to go and look at them. Then I came home from work to find that I had missed a call from SWEP asking if I was still willing to take Moon on as the new home had been deemed not right for her. They gave me a huge list of all her physical problems and a very short list of the things she was allowed to eat. Nothing was going to put me off, though, so Moon came to live with us. The clubbing stopped and I spent nearly all my time with her. However, the horse who had been so calm and quiet turned into a psychopath the day after she came to live with me; during my second ride on her she reared, resulting in me falling off and injuring my ribs. She refused to leave the yard by herself and threatened to rear if I tried to pretend I was brave enough to keep asking. When we did go out, she would half rear and spin round, and go back the way we had come. I had her teeth, back, saddle and health all checked out to eliminate physical problems. I was terrified of her and after she refused to load into the horsebox to come home from a show I was ready to give up. I decided on the six-mile walk back from the show that I was going to phone SWEP and tell them I couldn't cope. But something happened to stop me making that phone call.

My family and I went along to a SWEP animal communication day. Madeleine was the communicator there and she did readings for all the other dogs and horses that had been brought along, which were obviously very moving for all concerned. When it was my turn, I had no idea what to expect but Madeleine talked about all the physical issues that Moon had and we talked about some issues in my life with Moon. Suddenly, though, Madeleine started to cry and said she couldn't continue for now but would I stay behind afterwards, or ring her the next day. I was frightened about the reaction Madeleine had had, and terrified of making the call in case I was going to be told Moon was unhappy or I was doing something terribly wrong. I was not prepared for the information Madeleine was to give me. She told me that Moon and I had been together in a past life—I was a Native American and she was my horse. I had been killed while I was riding her and she felt guilty for not saving me. In this life, by refusing to leave the yard when I rode her and by spinning round and heading for home when she didn't feel safe, Moon was trying to protect me from being hurt again.

I went to the stables the next morning and gave Moon the biggest hug ever. I told her that I understood but although we had to protect each other, we could still have fun. We didn't look back from that day on. I was able to hack her out alone that weekend—OK, it wasn't all plain sailing, as Moon still spun round in fear a few times, but now that I understood why it was much easier to deal with. Through Madeleine I learned a lot more about Moon's history. She had been a hurdle racer until she had caught her hind legs on a hurdle, which pushed them upwards, bending her back the wrong way. This had caused her pelvis to rotate and trapped the nerves in front of it. Her racing career had to end, so she was sold to a dressage yard where they beat her because she physically couldn't work the way that they were asking her to. So she was sold again.

In April 2007 my granddad and I were in a car accident. Granddad was shaken but OK, but I had a painful neck and was taken to the local hospital. The bones in my neck were bent the wrong way and the third vertebra had been pushed out backwards and was squeezing my spinal column. The spinal specialists were all amazed that I was alive, let alone able to walk. I was unable to move my left arm for ten days and was in a neck brace for four weeks, but I still made it to the stables every day to be near Moon and my other pony Carrie.

Early in 2008, when Madeleine came out to see the horses, Moon's first words as she 'spoke' to Madeleine were "red car hurt my mum." Moon would not have been able to see the accident from her field. She gave Madeleine all the details of the accident and was very concerned, as she "didn't know what she would do if something happened to me." Things went from strength to strength in our relationship and in 2009, after months of hard work, Moon and I were awarded our first ever rosette for jumping. When she first came to live with me, Moon was terrified of even trotting over a pole on the floor and found it difficult to canter on the right lead, so we had certainly come a long way. She also grew more and ended up at 16.1hh.

On 29 July 2009, my granddad and I arrived at the yard to find Moon lying down in her stable. This was nothing unusual, but then as Granddad mixed up the feeds, Moon started to kick at her belly. I walked her around but she just kept getting worse and worse. The vet came, gave her two injections and then called another vet out for a second opinion. It took four of us to hold Moon upright so that the vet could listen to her heart rate. I was told her gut had twisted and that I had to make a decision: she could go to Bristol for an operation or I could choose to end her suffering. I couldn't begin to imagine how I was going to survive without my best friend, who had turned my life around and possibly even saved my life. I knew, though, deep down, that my beautiful mare would never make the three-hour journey in a trailer, and I made the decision. When the vets told me that she had gone, Moon sent a beautiful image into my mind: she was galloping free through a field of grass. I knew then that I had made the right decision.

What Madeleine had told me about my Native American past life stayed with me and I began doing research into past lives. I put my next decision off for a long time, but 2010 brought about a lot of changes for me and I decided that something was stopping me from moving forward in this life, and that now was the time to find out what I could about what might have happened in a past life to cause it. My regression brought out more than I had ever dreamed it could.

I walk down the stairs towards the door with bright light behind it, and as I go through the door I am immediately hit by the openness of my surroundings. I am all alone on a slight hill, apart from my horse who is standing to my right-hand side. My shoes are light brown in colour, made of leather with no straps, but with darker leather ties almost functioning as laces to hold them on. The rest of my clothes are also of the same light-brown leather, which I get the impression is deer or buckskin. In this life I am male and seventeen years old, with long dark straight hair and strong prominent cheekbones. It is daytime, and high summer; the grass is dry and yellowy brown. I have a white and black eagle feather tied vertically into the back of my hair with a leather thong. There are no other animals around, the sky is very blue and there is one bird high up in the sky. It is 1769.

I am overwhelmed by love for my horse when Madeleine asks me to describe her, and the feeling makes me cry uncontrollably. She is taller than all the other ponies and white with brown spots, including a large brown patch on her nearside shoulder. She has a blue circle around her eye and, I don't know at this point what this means, but I say to Madeleine that she "likes her red hand print on her shoulder." There are also other yellow-painted symbols on her body. Her name is Hanwei and she is wanted by all who see her but, I say to Madeleine, "She is with me." She is very fast and agile, able to turn right round from a flat-out gallop almost within her own body length, but she is fiercely loyal to me. My name is, I think, Elk, but I find it very hard sometimes to work out what English word I want. It is very difficult to speak at all at times as the words don't seem to want to form in my mouth. I am very afraid of someone taking Hanwei from me as she means the world to me. She is Moon, I'm convinced of it.

Madeleine asks what I was doing and I knew I was trying to find a village belonging to my enemies. I then had a flashforward to standing on a different hill, looking down at the village of the enemy tribe. The men are all standing together with lots of paint on them and, I say, 'They wear more paint than us.' There are a lot of people and I am afraid, as I know they will kill me if they find me. I felt they were the Choctaw and I was Oglala Sioux. I then flashed forward again to riding Hanwei along a high trail with lots of boulders around us. The trail is very narrow and the next thing I know, the enemy have pulled me off Hanwei and have hold of my arms. There are lots of men surrounding me and they are all shouting. I don't remember reaching the enemy village, but I wake up tied to a post with my arms behind my back. The men are still surrounding me and I can see Hanwei nearby; they are hurting her and pulling her about. She is frightened and rearing up, trying to get to me. The person is shouting at her and I can't understand what any of them are saying because they speak a different language to me. The men in front of me have now got a big knife with a wooden handle; they are all looking at it and talking until suddenly the knife is held to my throat and everything goes black. I am then able to look at myself from outside myself, tied to the post with my throat cut while the men dance and holler around my body. Hanwei is screaming and attacking the man holding her with her front hooves. I had waited too long watching the village; I was meant to be protecting my people but I have failed them. I didn't listen to my instinct or Hanwei, and if I had gone when she got fidgety, I would have survived.

I see my father sitting outside his tipi back in our village. His hair is greying and he is intimidated by me—he fears my abilities and what I can do. He is getting weaker now and fears me trying to take his place as chief, but I am not ready for that yet. I recognize his black eyes as those of a man I work with in my current life; a man who gives me the impression of being intimidated by me. My father told me to take others with me on this mission but I refused as I wanted to win Spotted Dove as my wife. She is beautiful and has eyes with a touch of green to them, which is unusual for my people. After I died, she married someone else and had three children. I could see her face vividly in my mind and it then receded, appearing smaller and smaller and disappearing into darkness. Her face made me smile and I heard her say, 'Tell Madeleine I know her. Tell her hello'.

A couple of weeks after my regression and a few days before the anniversary of Moon's death, I was meditating in bed before going to sleep and I started visualizing myself galloping on a horse. I could feel the horse's muscles moving beneath me and see my buckskin clothes as I looked down. I could see the ties holding my 'shirt' together and the blue lines painted on it. I then tried to look down at my horse, and was hit like lightning with an image of Moon. I could feel her energy filling me and I knew beyond doubt that it was her that I was riding. I don't know if I regressed again or if Moon was giving me a beautiful gift, but I spent a good five minutes feeling the joy of riding her. The sense of freedom I felt cannot be matched, nor can the love that she filled me with. I could feel my joy—I laughed as we galloped along, my arms outstretched. I was able to feel what was happening as well as being able to watch the scene from outside, like a film. Just because Moon is not here for me to physically touch and see, it doesn't mean that she is not still here in some way and sharing my life. Whenever I am feeling down, I get signs from Moon; for example, she blessed my decision to buy a new horse with my compensation money from the accident. My Arab filly Kalila had a regular-shaped star when I paid for her when she was four and a half months old, but by the time I brought her home, her star had turned into a crescent-moon shape. I know that Moon is still pushing me on to complete my life mission and I hope I can do her proud.

As for my past-life regression, I was fascinated by my glimpse of this previous life and did a lot of research into Native American culture. Many of the things that I found out chimed with what I had experienced during my regression; for example, my feeling that I had been part of the Sioux nation made sense as by the mid to late seventeenth century they were one of the most successful and prevalent nations in America. The feather that I had been wearing was of a kind that would have been awarded by the community's leaders –chieftains or war chiefs. A single upright feather like mine indicated that the warrior had achieved their first coup in war, which makes sense as in my regression I was still a young man.

My horse's eye was drawn around with a blue circle of the kind that was used as a sign that the horse was admired for its alert vision. My comment to Madeleine that my horse liked "her red handprint on her shoulder" relates to the fact I discovered that in Sioux culture red handprints on a horse's shoulder were celebrated in stories and legends about brave warriors both human end equine, and were much-prized 'battle scars'.

People of the Choctaw nation lived in the same area as the Sioux and they often clashed in battle. Choctaw men would paint their faces and bodies bright colours during battles, and some also wore tribal tattoos on their arms and legs. This sheds light on my comment "they wear more paint than us."

Lastly, and most incredibly I think, the name of my horse in my past life—Hanwei—means 'moon' in the Lakota language.

Sera realized that the 'blocks' that made it hard for her to go forward in her life were related to her past life with Moon. She had still been carrying guilt about not listening to her instincts and trusting her gut feelings, which was making her doubt her judgement and ability to choose the right career and make the right life decisions. How wonderful that she and Moon found each other again and, when we rewrote the script, journeyed through so much to bring about the resolution of 'Sera' in her male form of Elk—getting away and keeping his people safe and finding happiness by marrying Spotted Dove.

To this day, whenever I pop in to see Sera and her horses I am always met by an image of Moon, overseeing the proceedings and making sure Sera keeps on track with her self-belief.

CHAPTER 8

Why is it important to listen to our pets?

Above all, our animals want us to be empowered and to reach our full potential. It's as though when we're happy they're happy, so they work very hard to help us release anything that is no longer serving us and limiting our potential. As we come up against challenges in our lives, we can quite easily lose track of our core essence — our 'personal power', if you will. This can stem from events and situations in the past, such as negative comments, behaviour and messages sent by our peers at school or our family members during childhood. I see these negative messages and comments as sharp 'barbs' that go in very deep, causing pain and injury to our psyche and our belief systems. Later in life, challenges at work and problems in relationships can reinforce our perception of the 'self' that has already been formed in early life. The result of this is that over time we become disempowered. This is obviously connected to issues of self-doubt, but I feel that it also goes a lot deeper; I believe it is a process of whittling away or draining our strength of conviction, which causes increased disconnection to the 'I AM', or the sense of the divine within each one of us, and the deep-down knowledge that we are perfect just as we are.

Danny and Maria — Healing Your Past

The following case study is absolutely fascinating; it beautifully illustrates an inextricable link between an animal and a young woman. Their pasts were incredibly similar. It can only be that they found each other in order for them both to heal and to become re-empowered by their mutual support.

I was called out to see a stallion called Danny who had been displaying some very curious physical symptoms. He had developed a terrible cough and would stand with his front legs straddled apart, struggling to breathe.

This only happened at night when he was in his stable. He had been treated for common problems such as dust allergies, etc., with no success, and he was found to have a minor infection, but nothing on a scale that could explain the extent of his distress. A further puzzling thing about Danny's suffering and his distressing behaviour was that it also seemed to be emotional.

Before I met Danny I did a reading from a sample of his hair and picked up that he had a past life in which he had died in a barn fire. In his current life, when the coughing started he was the same age as he had been when he died in his past life. I went to see Danny and his owner asked me if I could also spend time with the young woman, Maria, who looked after him. I had got the impression from my veterinary friend who had referred Danny's case to me that Maria, who was now in her late twenties, had been in a sense 'adopted' by his owner's family a few years ago. Approaching Danny's stable door, I was immediately struck by the connection I could feel between him and Maria. I had been warned that Danny had previously 'jettisoned' unwanted visitors from his stable and that he detested vets and needles, so I worked very hard to reassure him that I had the utmost respect for him and that I was there to help. Maria handled Danny expertly, gently reassuring him that all was well—she scratched him in all his favourite places, which he adored. His magnificent mane cascaded from the crest of his regal neck, and his muscular chest commanded my deepest respect as he stomped his powerful hooves and lunged out with his teeth in defence of his personal space. I confess that this was a little daunting!

Being in Danny's presence was awe-inspiring—he was a magnificent creature. He allowed me to touch and scratch him as I sent him out as much love from my heart as I could, and slowly he began to communicate with me.

He started to 'tell' me that there were parallels between Maria and himself. I didn't understand what he meant, so I questioned his owner, who acknowledged that this was true. As I watched Danny and Maria interacting, I glimpsed their deep connection and the dynamic between them—it was as though they were healing each other on a deep level, as if through loving, reciprocal, physical contact they were both exorcizing their past demons. I thought that Danny had been bred by his current owner, so I had no idea at this point that he had any bad history. I discovered only later just how similar Danny and Maria's younger years had been.

I performed a 'soul retrieval' on Danny, bringing back the part of him traumatized and 'separated' by the terrible fire in his past life. I saw a holographic image of his past self and visualized 'blowing' the missing fragment of himself back into his physical body, which he courageously allowed me to do.

Maria was surprised at his reaction: he became much calmer and his eyes took on a softer expression. We discussed various remedies that the homoeopathic vet had prescribed and how the vet and I would work together to combine their findings and mine.

I then turned my attention to Maria. She seemed very reticent to agree to a session, but after seeing Danny be so accommodating and happy with my advances and subsequent healing session, she finally agreed. What followed was an incredible journey of courage and release. Using the NLP (neurolingustic programming) techniques of working with imagery and colour, I asked Maria to choose an image to represent her at this moment in time. This helps to externalize emotional pain and, when working and communicating with the image, greatly speeds up the healing process. It was obvious to me that there were some very deeply painful issues here, and Maria admitted that she found it very difficult to talk to or connect with anyone about herself; she only felt comfortable discussing horses, Danny in particular. Unsurprisingly, then, when we came to what appeared to be an immovable block of fear in the imagery, I was guided to bring Danny in to help. Using Danny's wisdom, advice and strength, Maria gradually found the courage to face her symbolic fear, which was very revealing of an extremely troubled past. Only with Danny's help could she begin to move forward and start to release her feelings of total disempowerment and fear.

As we used imagery techniques to work through Maria's chakra systems, she almost passed out when we connected to her solar plexus, which is the seat of self-belief. She became pale and almost seemed to diminish in size in front of me. I had never experienced such a dramatic reaction to this technique, but with Danny's help we managed to transmute the terrible negative visions into glowing, shining positive images, which immediately began to impact on Maria's energy. She grew in confidence as we discussed the implications of the transformative images, and she then divulged the extent of her humiliating abuse as a child, which had totally destroyed and disempowered her sense of self. Having had the courage to face her fears symbolically, she realized that this could be translated into starting to look at herself differently now, and that the possibility existed that she could be much more than she had previously thought, or been conditioned or allowed to think.

We discussed the possibility of Maria training to be a riding instructor, something that she desperately wanted to do but had no confidence in applying for, as she felt that she would only fail. I felt that she would have valuable insights into the confidence issues of her potential students and would be wonderful at allaying their concerns, because she would know exactly how it felt and how to give genuine reassurance and support.

Maria also revealed what a terrible past Danny had experienced in his previous homes. I understood that Danny hadn't told me about this as he wanted Maria to understand these 'parallels' he was talking about on a much deeper level.

Jane and Cat Dusty

This next reading was for a lady called Jane who was having serious relationship problems with her husband; he hated cats and forced Jane to make her cat, Dusty, sleep in the barn on their farm instead of in the house. Jane was becoming increasingly frustrated with her husband's lack of understanding about her beliefs and sensitivity to the needs of animals, and was feeling more and more guilty about the predicament she found herself in as she tried hard to make sure that Dusty was happy.

What a gorgeous cat! I always ask for a word or phrase that underpins the reading and what I get from Dusty is 'strength and purpose'. On an energy level he is extremely strong and was obviously determined to find you and be noticed by you. I feel as though you had no choice in the matter. Although I agree with what you say—his sight and hearing are not 100 percent—he uses all of his feline wiles and manages very well. I think these issues come from bad nutrition and possibly cat flu in his early life, which left him debilitated.

He has a big lesson to teach you about instincts and trusting your gut feelings. It feels very important that he is with you at this time, so let go of any guilt you have about this. It's a waste of energy! Accept the inevitable –this cat needs to be with you, so that you can learn from him what you need to know at this moment in time. His message is about renewed strength for you. This is potentially a very exciting time, but we all need to stand up for our beliefs and have the courage of our convictions, even if there is opposition from family and former friends. At first I know this can feel a little isolating, but when you remember who and what you are, you will start to attract the people, situations and animals that you need in your life now. We are all changing at such a profound level—our very DNA is changing. However not everyone is changing at the same rate and we all have to be allowed to take our own time and our own path. I know this might sound a bit like a lecture, but Dusty is very keen that I tell you this!! He wants very much to re-empower you, and this is connected to his skill at getting around despite the limitations of his outward senses—he wants you to 'feel' your way into things more, to see how they 'sit' with you before you do anything, and to know that you will always choose the right direction or course if you listen to your inner guidance.

It is no coincidence that Dusty has walked into your life at this point—it feels quite pivotal to you in your current incarnation. I feel you have had many lifetimes together and, as you say, he does have a sense of ownership of you, but I'd prefer to call it a vested interest! He wants you to be the very best you can be. Looking into his eyes, I can see several Egyptian past lives with you. He's telling me that you held positions of power over your ex-partner and that these issues were left unresolved and have carried on into this lifetime. Did you feel that this partner undermined your confidence or your beliefs? I can see Dusty as a temple cat and as a fellow priest, so he has experienced both sides of the coin. He's talking about an injury to your hands from that time—have you had any problems with your hands in this life? This is very connected with giving your power away, or perhaps having it forcibly removed, in the past.

I feel you are doing everything you can for him. You could try talking to a homoeopathic vet and think about giving him homoeopathic remedies instead of vaccinations. He certainly looks very healthy in his photos and I think he is very strong constitutionally. Don't worry too much about what you can do for him—it's more a case of what he wants to do for you!

I feel that he likes to check out the farm as he likes to stretch and exercise his inner senses, so I really don't feel there is anything to worry about. He seems very self-sufficient and wise to what you both need.

I feel that it's extremely important to understand that we all travel in soul groups and that often the people that are the most challenging for us to connect or interact with are in fact showing us the things in us that need to be healed. In the case of Jane and her husband, although they were not necessarily conscious of it, power struggles from their previous lives were definitely impacting on their relationship. They had come together once more to work through this unfinished soul contract.

The Dog That Cried Wolf!

This next case is fascinating: it shows that this lovely pet had chosen to be born with the challenge of deafness, which was directly connected to the trauma of hearing the terrible fate of his owners in their combined past life. Again this illustrates to me our pre-birth contracts and the agreements that are made on a soul level.

Harry came whirling into my healing room like a tan-and-white tornado. With his gangly legs, as he cavorted around in a state of high excitement, he looked like a Jack Russell on stilts. He seemed so pleased with himself and very happy to be with us. However, nothing that I verbalized made any difference to him: Harry was born stone deaf. Telepathically though, he could 'hear' me, and he was overjoyed to be able to babble away, having a two-way conversation with me, explaining why he was behaving in his somewhat annoying, whinging way. His lovely owner Laura said that he had seemed to have accepted being left alone, but if she was at home and Harry was shut in somewhere, say behind a door in the kitchen, he would have something to say about it! If he could see through the house from front to back he seemed much calmer. It was as though he was only happy when he had a clear view of whatever might be happening right throughout the house. I considered the fact of his deafness and how this might be connected to his whinging, as I'd noticed that my old terrier Teazle, now that she was going deaf, seemed much more clingy than she had been and would howl mournfully if I was out of sight—if I was just in the next room, or in the loo, she would not let up. The only way to stop her howling was to let her come to the loo with me—obviously there could be no privacy in our house! I felt with both Harry and Teazle that, because they couldn't hear their human carers, they felt they couldn't monitor them properly, and although Harry had a carefree exterior, I thought that underneath he was a sombre little dog who took his duties very seriously. The reason for this began to unfold as he was courageous enough to start to show me a very traumatic past life where his current owners had been his parents. Harry's reason for finding his way back to these people, his soul companions, started to become clear as Harry communicated with me.

Just a few days before our session, Laura had had a very unpleasant dream in which she felt that she was being pursued and that she would come to a sticky end, threatened and then attacked by big knives. Her partner had also been experiencing nightmares about being chased and awoke many a night feeling very fearful. I had known nothing of these dreams until Harry started to tell me about their shared past-life trauma.

He started by saying that no one would believe him and no one appreciated just how much he wanted to protect Laura. He talked of a time in Cambodia under a regime reminiscent of Pol Pot's, where genocide was rife. Harry (in his incarnation as a young boy) was renowned for telling lies and exaggerating to get attention, so much so that no one ever knew if he was telling the truth or not. When I told Laura this, she said that there was a young boy within her current life who was prone to using these 'cry wolf' tactics, and how much it unnerved her.

In Cambodia one day, the boy Harry had come rushing into their hut shouting that the enemy tribe were coming and they must get away. Because he had told so many lies in the past, though, his parents ignored him. But, just as in the tale of the boy who cried wolf, this time he was telling the truth.

What happened next was horrific. Harry never again wanted to hear terrible sounds like those he heard as his parents were killed with machete-like weapons. It was hardly a surprise that he had chosen to come back without hearing. While I was relaying what Harry was telling and showing me, Laura became quite emotional; she was beginning to get pictures in her mind from Harry. I asked him to show Laura what they had all looked like and the layout of their home, so that Laura could tune in in order for us all to change the outcome and heal the trauma once and for all.

Harry's body language was fascinating. When he was describing the awful scenes unfolding, and the emotions he felt, he sat right in front of me with his gaze fixed on my face, really boring into my mind in his desperation to be 'heard'. As soon as Laura started to work with us he ran over to her, and stared right into her face as she visualized the scenes that he was showing her. Harry guided us both as I 'shadowed' or followed along as they played out the new outcome where, this time, the family heeded Harry's warning and escaped to safety. I didn't say anything out loud about what I was getting from Harry; I wanted to be sure that Laura was picking up from him exactly how they were to escape. They managed to creep out through a reed panel at the back of their hut and run as fast as they could away from the approaching men. Because Harry had in the past done a lot of hiding from his parents and the rest of the villagers (in case they tried to make him do chores!) he knew all the best places to hide. He took them to a marshy area, where they had to hide almost beneath the water line. They had to stay there for a long time, but finally they managed to get away safely and eventually came to another, bigger village, where they were made welcome and protected.

Laura felt a huge sense of relief and I asked her to concentrate on and expand that feeling, thanking Harry for his help and telling him what a great dog he was and how brave he'd been.

Happily, Harry is much calmer these days and, although still protective, he doesn't seem to fret nearly as much. Laura and her partner say that they feel calmer as well. They are so happy to know that their wonderful dog cares so much for them.

The final case in this chapter expands further on this theme and illustrates the concept of how multi-dimensional — and extraordinary — we all are.

Cynthia and Bonito/Ben

I first encountered Cynthia and Bonito a few years ago. He is a stunning dark-bay Hanoverian horse and was bred to perform top-class dressage, which is why Cynthia bought him. However, this has never quite happened, much to her frustration — he would show glimpses of genius and then, as Cynthia puts it, 'the brakes go on'. I recorded his story in my first book *An Exchange of Love*, as he was the first horse to teach me the visualization technique of using etheric 'light crystals', which we have also seen in Belle and Fiona's case, in disc form to help with back pain in horses and their owners.

Bonito was very nervous when I came to see him the first time; he was worried that I might be a prospective buyer as he had been moved on several times in his life. We have had several sessions, peeling back more 'onion' layers in each one, and finally he was brave enough to show us what was really going on. Cynthia adores Bonito and had been getting more and more heartbroken as they kept failing to recapture and build on their moments of brilliance together, and the bliss of when horse and rider completely merge and you become as one.

The following is an account of a very profound past-life healing session between Cynthia and me, which we felt paved the way for the final unravelling of Bonito's previous incarnations and the deep connection between horse and owner.

When Cynthia emailed me a picture of Ben, a horse she had owned in the past who had caused her severe injury and sadness, I was amazed at how much like Bonito he looked. We had said before that they could have been the same horse, but this session revealed the meaning of this and the extent to which Bonito wanted to heal the past. As I drove to the yard, I telepathically asked Bonito to help us as much as he could and told him that I sincerely wanted to help relieve him of everything that was holding him back from truly enjoying his life with Cynthia, and when I arrived he seemed very bright and eager to commence the session. Bonito first asked me to ask Cynthia to look at his back to see if there were any patterns that needed addressing, but as she went to lay her hands on him, he laid his ears right back and grumpily told me to tell her that she should use just her eyes and her intuition, not her hands!

Amazing resemblance: Ben and Bonito (right)

Cynthia found some issues and Bonito told me to ask her to visualize that she was working on Ben's back. While she was doing this Bonito did some huge stretches, lengthening his spine. He then asked me to allow Cynthia to tune in to the part of her body that was seriously injured when she had her fall with Ben, and to send forgiveness to both herself and Ben for these traumas. She did so easily and her pain seemed to lessen considerably. What follows is Cynthia's side of the story; it is testament to her undying love for her horses and the craving to understand just how incredible our connections are with our animals and just how much they want us to be healed by them.

Cynthia is trained in craniosacral therapy and her account of the past-life regression session we had makes reference to this healing modality, which works with the body's natural capacity for self-repair. The craniosacral system has an inherent rhythmic motion, which can be felt as a subtle tide gently ebbing and flowing and manifesting in all body tissue. Disturbances to health and well-being on any level will disturb the flow of the tide and certain energetic patterns will form; in craniosacral therapy these patterns are gently encouraged to resolve, enabling the body to process and heal the associated physical and/or emotional disturbance.

Cynthia's account of her regression is extraordinarily detailed and vivid, and the changes it has helped her and Bonito to make are quite astonishing.

As Madeleine explained that we were going to work through the chakras and see what emerged, I silently asked Flight, a beloved horse of mine who has passed on, to come and help me, and I felt her energy come in over my left shoulder. My base chakra was a purple whirl, relaxed and steady, forming into a tunnel moving away from me. My sacral chakra was a yellowy-green—it seemed to be approaching me, and was big and bright, but if I tried to look into it, it retreated and became a purple-red whirl. I then saw the nose and the head of a lioness against a yellow background. The solar plexus chakra contained a whole plethora of colours, and at this point Bonito gently placed his head on my shoulder, which felt wonderfully cuddly. A golden-pink glow emerged, which seemed to be absorbing me, then flowers came up from the centre—red roses—and I felt very loved. My heart chakra was red with large red flowers and a yellow-and-purple mist emerging from it. Then I began to feel cold as a white mist appeared, and from a red-and-pink whirl of energy Eliza, another of my horses, appeared, telling me to keep my head up. Eliza stayed with me for quite some time, with her nose in my hands. Her energy was very strong and powerful and in her neck I could see a small foal lying down with its head up, looking at me. I knew the foal was me as Eliza had told us before that I had been her foal in a past life. She had come to give me maternal love and support. Bonito appeared, as though inspecting me. A unicorn nodded to me, indicating, I felt, that all was well, and I could see more red flowers. A white horse put its third eye against mine. It felt wonderful; everything was white and a crystal valley opened up in front of me. At the throat chakra I could see the head of a stocky grey horse with a shining white nose. Then I saw a coil of rope and the grey horse reared up, looking frightened and agitated. A mist came down and a tunnel opened up through the grey horse's eye. Looking through a golden glow I could see distant mountains, wagons and horses. I was riding a dark horse and went flying up through the air. Suddenly everything became disconnected. Bonito stood with his head in front of mine as though he was trying to protect me from something, but I asked him to move, knowing that whatever it was I had to face it. I was shown a black-and-white picture of a man hanging from a rope over a stone railway bridge. As the rope was attached to a vehicle and the body hauled back over the bridge, I knew that this man was me. In total despair I had put a rope round my neck and thrown myself over the bridge, leaving my horses feeling totally abandoned.

Through Madeleine, the archangel Michael asked that I use the sword of truth to cut the ties with this past life, which were holding me back in my current life. I took the sword of truth and cut the rope from round my neck. I instantly felt as though I was jumping into the future, doing things I had never dreamed of and feeling very happy. Bonito came to me with a golden glow around him, telling me to have confidence in the future. I could feel myself going down a golden tunnel, towards a golden future. Everything felt wonderful.

To help the pain and stiffness that I suffered from in my neck, Madeleine performed some sound healing with a singing bowl. Archangel Michael was at Madeleine's shoulder guiding the tone and pitch as she used the crystal bowl and the soothing healing energy that came into my neck felt wonderful.

A few days after the session the emotion of it caught up with me, and I felt huge sorrow and regret at having abandoned my horses. I desperately wanted to know what had happened to them after I had left them. Madeleine suggested that I engage in the practice of rewriting the script—I was to visualize my horses talking me out of it and all of us walking off together, a happy little group. Although I had always understood rewriting the script to be a powerful process, I was sceptical as to whether it was going to work for me, because my sorrow and regret for my horses were running very deep. But nevertheless I lit a candle and visualized the rewritten script, and much to my amazement I felt very happy as we all walked off together into a better future.

About six weeks later I was again experiencing some neck pain and stiffness. I assumed this to be another layer emerging from the past-life-changing episode, so I contacted Madeleine for some distance healing. A couple of days later I took Bonito to a dressage competition. Bonito has stunning paces but has not come near to fulfilling his dressage potential, and has not shown much inclination to try to do so. He had regularly displayed what could only be described as 'attitude', and from such a highly evolved sensitive soul as I know him to be, this apparent contradiction and unhappiness has always bothered me. We had by this time acquired a wonderful dressage trainer who taught us a lot, and had seemingly endless knowledge and certainly endless patience, but my intuition was telling me 'Three's a crowd', so I reluctantly stopped the dressage training, knowing deep down that Bonito and I needed to be alone to resolve some fundamental issues between us. I continued with our schooling sessions, trying to ride Bonito lightly and intuitively. Occasionally we felt as one, but more often than not there was something between us, something blocking us, that I felt needed resolution.

As I drove Bonito to the dressage competition I knew that, unlike other competition days, this time I could stand back emotionally. I would be able to remain centred, detached from the desire to win or get points. Bonito didn't want to go in the arena—it was as though he was experiencing stage fright—and when we eventually started our dressage test, riding him was like driving a car with the handbrake on!

Driving home, though, I was not unhappy; in fact I felt quite pleased. Standing back from what had been happening had enabled me to realize that what was standing between us was Bonito's incarnation as Ben, and the time was right for this to be resolved. Just to confirm this, the neck pain that I had been experiencing was now reaching the point in my back that I had injured during my first serious fall on Ben.

I asked Madeleine for a session with Bonito and he started by showing her a picture of a tangled ball of string, which is how he felt about his life as Ben; he readily acknowledged that he had messed it up. He explained how difficult it is to be incarnated as a horse, with no control over where you go and what you do. He talked about his frustration that humans don't understand the suffering and unhappiness they can cause if they are un-aware of just how sensitive horses are. As a foal he had experienced a very insensitive weaning, and had missed his mother greatly. He was then put with two other horses and relied on them totally for support, but very soon he was taken away from them and transported from Ireland to England. As a youngster he was subjected to treatment that he described as brutal, and went through an auction that made him feel traumatized. I bought him as a four-year-old and had thought him to be a very self-contained, confident youngster, not appreciating the trauma and insecurity that lay just beneath the surface. I wasn't able to provide sufficient support for him and eventu-ally, as his frustration and anger surfaced, two serious accidents ensued. I had never stopped loving Ben and had always wished that I had been able to find an answer to his problems. Bonito asked me to send both him and myself huge waves of forgiveness.

He then asked me to resolve, in craniosacral therapy terms 'patterns', some problems or issues on both himself and on his form as Ben. In effect, Bonito courageously stepped aside and allowed me to access the essence of Ben so that I could work on him. Bonito asked how I felt about being unfairly judged by others, and asked me to reflect on situations in my life when this had happened. I said that all I really wanted when I rode him was a feeling of being at one with each other, and that if we could achieve that feeling, it really didn't matter to me how anyone else judged us. I just wanted the thrill of experiencing poetry in motion with him. Madeleine then suggested that we rewrite the script, and for me to visualize mounting Ben and starting our ride as I had done at the time of the accident, but this time to ride him successfully and happily. I did that very easily, and felt that all had been forgiven. We understood each other very deeply now.

Through Madeleine, I asked Bonito how he would like me to ride him, and he said he wished to be ridden exactly as I had just ridden Ben in the visualization.

Over the next few days, Bonito was a pleasure to ride. I built our school-ing sessions up gradually, making sure that I was coming from the place deep within me where I had been able to make contact with Ben. In those early sessions I worked only in walk and trot. I felt very strongly that I need-ed to visualize cantering on Ben before I asked Bonito to canter.

The first time I visualized cantering on Ben, his canter was disunited; in other words his legs were moving in the wrong sequence. This startled me because it was the reason why one of Bonito's previous owners had insisted that he have surgery on his spine. I visualized some more craniosa-cral work with Bonito, then visualized riding him again. This time his canter was correct, but there was still room for improvement as he was much better balanced on one rein (side) than the other. In my next visualization I 'saw' good dressage canters on both reins, but I kept turning into a race jockey, racing Ben over fences, which made me believe that Ben had been holding on to these injuries from an incarnation as a racehorse. I was also sure that I had been his jockey—no wonder I was still having so many aches and pains!

Exactly a week after Madeleine's visit I took Bonito out for a schooling session, knowing that the time was right to ask for some canter work. I had a deep inner confidence, but still an outer layer of anxiety. Difficulty establishing and maintaining canter had been one of the early signs of my deteriorating relationship with Ben, and was also an issue with Bonito. We were at one in walk and trot; it felt wonderful and I almost didn't want to spoil it by asking Bonito for canter. It would be a serious test for both of us. I tried to feel confident as I gently asked him for canter. The result was stunning—a powerful, wonderful canter that needed just a tiny adjustment to become a canter of dressage quality. We felt incredible together.

The next step will be to achieve this in competition, but one of the most important things I have learnt is that, if that joy of being together is compromised in any way, I simply have to go back to Ben to work again on resolving and healing the issues.

My horses have guided me through some amazing experiences, and have awakened me spiritually in a way that has totally transformed my life.

It amazes me, when I think back to my sessions with Cynthia and Bonito, to think of how these processes work. Bonito brought in his past incarnation as Ben so that everyone involved could have their past-life issues healed on many levels, which in turn brought about the forgiveness and healing that both he and Cynthia so craved and needed in this lifetime.

CHAPTER 9

Do our pets resent being euthanized?

"Death does not come as an end, it comes as a friend.
Our bodies are only shells left on the shores of life;
on the oceans of light the vessels of spirit and love never die"
ROSE DE DAN, *TAILS OF A HEALER*

This of course is a very distressing subject and one that I am frequently asked about. I felt it was important to include this issue here, as obviously it can affect anyone who has animals. I have found these occasions extremely painful and difficult, and have suffered enormous guilt at the memory of my beloved pet's passing. I remember an old farmer friend of our family saying in a very matter-of-fact way, "When you've got live animals, you've got dead animals!" As a child I'd thought this a rather callous attitude, but I understand far more now, having been educated by the animals themselves. One of my most important animal teachers is Pillow, my dog in spirit. She has taught me so much about the wasted energy of the emotion of guilt and has explained to me that animals have a much better understanding of death and dying than we humans usually do. She emphasized that animals—and people—who pass on are never truly lost and tells me off if I ever use phrases such as 'lost through cancer'. She drums it into me that everything is healed in spirit and that it is just another dimension, to be thought of almost as just stepping into another room. When I tried to explain to my son that our beloved goat Mulberry was going to have to be euthanized, because she was old and in severe pain, I asked for Pillow's guidance so that I could find the best words to help him understand that his best friend and confidante could no longer be with us in a physical form. I told him that just as we are responsible for the optimum well-being of the life of the pets in our care, if we are truly caring owners we also have to be just as responsible when it comes to their death. I fully believe that animals tell us when they are ready to pass. With Mulberry I felt sure, but needed some extra guidance, because there was so much personal emotion surrounding the profound connection she had with my little boy. I consulted a wonderful animal communicator, Julie Dicker, who has now triumphantly passed to spirit to perform even greater feats of healing. Julie tuned in to Mulberry and concurred that it was definitely the right thing to do. I also told my son that whatever happened, the love that they'd felt for each other in their extraordinary relationship would be in his heart forever. We had a wonderful final weekend with lots of cuddles and special titbits and after we had made the decision, our lovely goat appeared very happy and even cuddlier than she normally was. My son did seem to understand, and he hated the thought of his goat friend being in pain. In fact he seemed to manage his emotions better than I did when the time came; he was so brave.

I remember clearly that after Mulberry had been put to sleep, I'd had to compose myself to help out a friend who was on an energy healing course and needed to practise on me. She completely understood my distressed state, but said she felt that a session might help. As I lay on her therapy couch, eyes closed, I was astounded to see a vivid image of Mulberry leaping up from the spot where she had died, with a whole new young body, and proceed to 'prong' around the yard like an overactive gazelle! When she was younger, if she was happy or excited, she would frantically wag her tail, and she was doing this again in the vision that she had sent me. I believe she sent this to show me how happy she was to be free of her old, painful body. I also know that she and my son have been together before in a previous life, and that they will find each other again when the time is right. For now, my son still feels her presence and checks in with her for guidance; her love has always been and always will live in his heart.

One of the more difficult aspects of my work is being asked if an animal is ready to pass, as owners struggle with the decision of whether to end their pet's life. Of course this is always very emotional, as I know exactly how they are feeling. When I tune in to the animal on a soul level, they give me very clear directives. Often they are anxious about the distress the situation is causing their human carer and, like Mulberry, they seek to find a way to reassure them that all is as it should be. Of all the readings I have performed with animals in spirit, I have never had an animal blame their owner for making these decisions; time and time again they remind me of the bigger picture—a soul-level overview to remind us, as Pillow reminds me, "Nothing is ever lost!"

Of course, it is important that we honour our grieving processes and allow ourselves to express these painful emotions when any loved one passes. It is those of us left behind who are filled with the heartache and the lack of the joy that their physical presence brought to our lives. I hope that the following stories help to ease a little of the pain that many of you have experienced.

Rachel and Emily

I had visited Rachel in order to communicate with her horse, but had been treated to a show of affection from her two huge and very friendly Rottweilers. Rachel had mentioned that one of the dogs, Emily, suffered from terrible fits and that she was concerned about controlling them as they were becoming far more frequent. Later, I was called to see Emily after she had had a very severe fit and had banged her head quite badly, causing much distress to the family. Rachel wondered if the best thing would be to have her euthanized. I felt that she was not quite ready, even though Emily 'told' me that she left her body during these severe fits and that she was finding it increasingly difficult to be in a physical form. I thought that Emily was in her way preparing her humans for the inevitable, and indeed a few months later I received another call from Rachel saying that Emily had suffered many fits that weekend and was lying in the driveway and appeared to not be properly in her body. I tuned in to Emily and got a very swift answer that she was ready to go, so Rachel called the vet and Emily took a deep breath and slipped away. While this was happening, Emily 'told' me that she wanted the family to celebrate their life together and that she wanted to spend time with them around her, almost as though she were lying in state. She showed me images of flowers and candles, so I explained the images to Rachel and suggested that she might like to perform a ritual with the children to show their love for Emily. Rachel later sent me the most beautiful photograph of Emily lying surrounded by rose petals and pictures that the children had drawn. Her other dog was lying with her and their black cat was also cuddling in. Emily looked regal and serene, as though she was relishing all the reverence she was receiving. When I tuned in to her she showed me her lovely wiggly bottom and short tail wagging, sending ripples up through her whole body—she was so happy! When I told Rachel, she said that Emily had only been able to do this when she was younger and that her whole body used to wag. Of course her physical form is sorely missed, but everyone in the family still feels her reassuring presence. I also felt that it was very healthy and valuable for the children to be able to make their contribution by drawing pictures in honour of their beloved Emily.

There is a school of thought that we should not try to hang on to people or animals who have passed, that we need to let them go so that they, and we, can move on. I do think this is true to a point, but I believe that our animals (and we, for that matter) can all become so multi-dimensional that we can choose to 'drop' in and out of many realities, as well as taking on new bodies to enable us to physically return to our loved ones.

Beautiful Bella

I had a similar case of reassuring messages and images from a beautiful horse called Bella.

Bella was shared by two people, who cared for her lovingly. However, Bella had been chronically lame for a long time and was only getting worse despite their best efforts. I did a reading at the request of one of her owners, who was very open to seeing things on a soul level, and it was clear from the reading that they had spent a previous life together. Obviously Bella's owner had a very deep connection to her and was going to find her passing very distressing, but when she contacted me again and said that the other owner had finally made the decision to put Bella down, I felt that it was the right thing to do and so it was agreed. At the time when I knew the vet had been scheduled to euthanize Bella, I was walking my dogs. I was visualizing sending Bella and her lovely owner healing white light in order to support them. Just after the scheduled time Bella came charging into my thoughts, bucking and squealing, galloping full pelt around the most beautiful meadow. She looked so happy and she gave me an overwhelming feeling of freedom. As soon as I got home, I emailed her owner to share what Bella had shown me and got a phone call back almost immediately. As soon as Bella had fallen she had sent the exact same image to her, so she too had witnessed the joy that Bella felt at being released from her pain. Although the whole thing was of course still very sad, we couldn't help but feel happy for Bella.

Frodo the Terrier

The next case illustrates the overwhelming power of the love we can receive from spirit, and raises the question of who might be waiting there to meet and guide our loved ones when they pass. It was a great comfort to us all to know that this wonderful dog was met and cared for in the gentlest of hands.

I was asked to call in to see a lady called Lorna. She wanted me to try to tune in to her old terrier Frodo, who had passed just three weeks previously, after she had made the final decision to have him put to sleep. He had battled cancer for a couple of years previously, twice having a large tumour removed from his side, but sadly it had returned viciously and this time he would not have been able to cope with the lengthy surgical procedure needed to remove it. He was fifteen years old and had had a lifetime of adoration from his owner.

As I sat looking at the photographs taken of Frodo the day before he died, and then one taken an hour before the vet had come, I was struck by the expression on his lovely furry face. Lorna was beating herself up about whether she should have had him operated on for a third time, and Frodo had been so stoic and courageous; I could see the struggle in his eyes, but he had been determined to keep going as long as he could in order to be strong for Lorna. I felt that it would have been cruel to put him through another operation, and I doubted whether he would have survived the anaesthetic. Looking at his last photo I could see in his eyes that he'd had enough. As I tuned in, Lorna asked me to find out if he'd been in pain. Frodo told me that the tumour had been just cumbersome at first, but as it progressed it had become painful. He then said that the timing of his passing had been perfect to the second. When I said this out loud, the whole of my body shivered, like a cold streak going through me. When this happens I always know that what I've just said is an absolute truth, so I felt happy to share Frodo's message with Lorna, as I hoped it would reassure her that she had absolutely done the right thing, honouring both Frodo and her own gut feelings. Whilst we were talking, Frodo kept showing me a larger black dog, who I felt was a female, running round him wagging her tail. Frodo also showed me lots of playful things that he could do now that he was in spirit, just like he used to do in his youth when he was fit and healthy. Lorna verified everything I passed on, and laughed as she remembered Frodo's antics. Lorna told me that she'd felt very sad not to have felt him at all since his passing, but that both her young children had experienced incredibly vivid dreams where they'd seen Frodo charging around them playing, just like he used to, which helped them to believe and accept that Frodo was happy and healthy in spirit. Frodo told me that Lorna was so exhausted and grief-stricken that her aura was almost in tatters. So we discussed some remedies that she could try and I told her that after this session with Frodo I would work to repair and strengthen her aura.

Lorna wanted to know who had been there in spirit to welcome Frodo, so I told her about the black dog. She identified her as a dog called Mandy who they'd owned a few years before. Mandy had been a very loving and gentle dog and Lorna was pleased that Mandy was there for Frodo. This wasn't all, however; Frodo then showed me his head being held between the gentlest, most compassionate hands I think I've ever seen. They were an older man's hands—I could see evidence of a little arthritis and an old-fashioned signet ring engraved with initials. Above all, it was the energy of these hands that was so striking; although they were a man's hands, and very masculine in appearance, they emanated great kindness and strength. The love that came through the hands into Frodo and then to reach Lorna completely overwhelmed me. As I described the hands and the ring, Lorna said "It's my grandfather!" He was so pleased to be acknowledged that he sent out a further wave—well, tsunami, actually!—of love for her. That was enough for me and I crumpled unashamedly into tears. Lorna and I both sat and blubbed, feeling so happy that Frodo was in such good hands—literally!

Sometimes, in contrast to the three cases above, I get a very clear answer from animals who tell me that they are not ready to go. They feel that they have yet more work to do and need more time to continue that work and that they still need to be here in the physical. It is vital that we endeavour to listen to our animals' needs. In one case I saw, a dog called Rosie had been booked into the surgery to be put to sleep, but the owner was still full of doubt. I consulted with holistic vets about her condition, and they suggested alternative treatment. Rosie made a full recovery and lived happily for two more years, when she passed peacefully all by herself. The owner's intuition had been absolutely right.

Even knowing all this, when my animals grow old and the time comes, I know it will still be very hard to make these decisions, and I know how hard it is for everyone faced with this question. I hope that reading this book has brought some small comfort to readers that our animals will always find a way to come back to us physically or support us from spirit on our life journeys.

CHAPTER 10

Meditations and visualizations to connect with the past and future lives of your pets

Love and respect are the two most important things to remember when communicating with your beautiful pet; respect them and never underestimate their wisdom. Animals very often feel and understand the deep, almost spiritual, connections we have with them. It never ceases to amaze me how aware they are of our physical and emotional issues, and how much they love to help us in making sure we are as happy and healthy as possible. Through their behaviour patterns they very often 'mirror' things that are going on in our lives; they may even take on physical symptoms in sympathy and a desire to help us. It follows that it is only right that we should be just as vigilant about them. By learning to listen to their needs and hear their advice we can learn a great deal about ourselves. We have to remember that even in the unassuming physical form of dogs, cats or guinea pigs, they are hugely complex beings and they care deeply about us.

Top Ten Tips for Communicating With Your Pet

- Either out loud or telepathically in your mind, ask, with the deepest respect, permission to connect with the animal. It may feel strange at first, but rest assured that they will 'hear' and understand you. Remember, pets know a lot more than we think they do!
- Before you start to try to hear what animals are 'saying', sit quietly and connect with your heart centre. It might help to close your eyes, so that you can really concentrate and focus on your task. Feel your heart opening like a beautiful bloom and imagine sending a silver or golden line, or beam of light, to connect with the heart centre of your pet.

- If you are just starting and want to practise, start with something simple, like asking about their favourite food or friend, or a favourite place they like to spend time in. It might be useful to have a notepad and pen to jot down whatever comes to mind as you learn to strengthen and build confidence about your telepathic skills.
- Remember that we all have these skills within us. Just starting to write what-ever comes into your head can help you prove this to yourself. What comes into your head may take the form of pictures, or look rather like a video clip of the animal's experiences. You may also experience physical feelings, sounds, smells or even tastes.
- If you feel any physical discomfort, for example toothache if the animal's teeth need attention, or backache if their back needs realigning, make sure you imagine breathing out the feelings down into the ground and out of your body; you don't want to be carrying around their discomfort.
- Think about whether the discomfort is in an area of *your* body that you have been ignoring, as your pet may be telling you to look after yourself.
- Your pet will know what mood you're in before you get up in the morning, so always feel free to discuss your problems with them — they make great shoulders to cry on. Sharing your problems will help your pet understand what's going on in your world and will alleviate their concern, as otherwise when they intuit that there's a problem they may think it's their fault. Also, just by talking your problems over, your pet may support you to encourage solutions to pop into your mind.
- Commit to an action plan so that you can see clearly how you can help your pet by aiming for a positive outcome to any issues. This will deepen your connection further, and build even more trust between you.
- Keep a journal of your impressions. Messages that may have not made sense at the time may begin to unfold in your understanding. Also if you are practising with other people's pets, it is useful to be able to tell them about impressions and thoughts so that they can verify the information you receive intuitively from your animal friends.
- Practise! Be confident and open to experiencing more balance, harmony and love between you and your pet than you ever thought possible. Remember — they have so much to teach us if we can just allow ourselves to listen.

This last tip is so important that it needs to stand outside the list: the most crucial thing of all is that you sincerely thank your pet for their patience, love and commitment. Their support is worth everything; it can help you reconnect with the wonders of the Universe and your individual, and our collective, divine purpose.

Winnie

When working with animals, it nearly always gets emotional, especially when it involves decisions about their lives and deaths, as discussed in the previous chapter. We have to master the ability to detach from extreme emotions if possible, in order to be more effective and to really help the situation. When contacting your spirit animals, allow yourself to feel only joy and the blessing of sharing your life with this beautiful creature and being loved by it. Before we move on, my lovely dog Winnie has reminded me to tell you about a gift that she gave a group on one of my animal communication courses. This was held at a wonderful venue belonging to Hoofbeats, a charity that takes in abandoned, neglected and unwanted horses and ponies. The horses have always been wonderful, helping people remember how to communicate with them and supporting people so that they can grow in confidence. Often a horse will give each group member a message, which is a real honour, especially if the horse has previously been poorly treated through cruelty or ignorance. On these occasions I am always blown away by the animals' capacity for forgiveness and compassion for us. On this course at Hoofbeats, we were asked to communicate with the most beautiful old horse, Dazzle. She had been brought into the sanctuary a couple of days before and anyone could see that she was a very sick horse indeed. She apparently came from a loving home that could no longer afford to care for her, but it seemed that her owners' ignorance had prevented them from realizing just how much she was suffering. I felt that she was near death and that she was getting ready to pass, and we all gave her love and healing as best we could. Some of the group were struggling as we shared the feelings we received from Dazzle. My rescue dog Winnie, who often 'co-facilitates' my courses, interrupted my thoughts by telling me that she wanted us all to go back into the lecture room as she had something to share with us. She gave us instructions to help us cope, 'telling' us to visualize a shape like a Native American dreamcatcher in front of our hearts. We were to visualize the weblike framework woven with crystals, filtering out any pain and catching it before it entered our hearts too deeply, which would prevent us from functioning effectively and being of service to the animals. This was not to stop us feeling and empathizing, but to maximize the flow of love inwards and outwards. Everyone felt much stronger after using this visualization and were able to return to Dazzle and continue giving her healing and love. Sharon, the wonderful director of the sanctuary, made the decision to have Dazzle put to sleep two days later. Some members of the group felt that we'd failed her as we hadn't managed to 'cure' or 'save' her, but I felt that it had been an honour for us to witness the last few days of Dazzle's life, knowing that she was so loved and that perhaps we had helped her pass with as much grace and peace as she deserved. Our pets do not want us to feel sad and suffer the agonies of grief. They want us to remember how much fun we had together and to celebrate our shared lives. Just as with human spirits, the spirits of animals can find it difficult to come through to us if they feel that it will upset us, so it's important to remember the love above all.

How, exactly, do we go about communicating with our animals? The list below sets out some of the forms by which we can connect with them. You may find that you are communicating in one of these ways, or several. There is no right or wrong way, and one is not better than another. The method of communication I experience with each animal varies, depending on what the particular animal is trying to help me understand. It's important to be open and allow whatever impressions come your way to show themselves to you. Trust your intuition!

Different ways of connecting with animals

- CLAIRVOYANCE: This literally means 'clear seeing' and refers to the ability to see images and pictures in your mind's eye. It also refers to the ability to intuitively know something about the past, present or future without any logical explanation as to why you would know it.
- CLAIRSENTIENCE: This means 'clear feeling' and refers to the ability to intuitively feel the emotions or physical feelings of another.
- CLAIRAUDIENCE: This means 'clear hearing' and refers to the ability to hear words and phrases in your 'mind's ear'. It is also known as telepathy. When you hear this way, the words and phrases may sound as if they're being said in your own voice, which can make you question what you're hearing, but you will with time and practice learn to trust your abilities.
- CLAIRALIENCE: This means 'clear smelling' and is not as common as some of the other forms, but some people do operate in this way and get very clear impressions of smells.
- CLAIRAMBIENCE: This means 'clear tasting' and is the intuitive ability to get impressions of taste. An example would be asking a cat to tell you her favourite food and getting an impression of the taste of fish!

You can also try to intuit the past and future lives of your pets in spirit by working with a photograph, a collar or perhaps your pet's ashes. Of course this can feel very emotional, but it can be wonderful to be given an image of what your lovely pet might return as. If you feel tearful, try to be joyful and remember that it is because you are feeling again the love that you shared with your pet. I perform countless readings for bereaved owners who pray that their pet has a soul and that they may one day return in a physical form. I am always so humbled when I am able to relay reassuring messages from these beloved animals. It's all the more powerful, though, if you can communicate with your pet yourself.

Years ago, I used to paint animal portraits. Sometimes owners would ask me to paint the pet that had died, and I would feel huge pressure to make sure that the likeness was the best it could be. I can remember staring at a photo struggling to capture a particular feature of a dog or other pet, and to my amazement I would feel the animal's spirit come into my energy field and, lo and behold, the portrait was complete. This happened many times and the eyes in the portrait would then have a new depth to them that I had previously been unable to capture. It was as though the pet wanted to come through me to be able to shine out and reassure their owners that their love was undying. Very often I would feel flooded and overwhelmed by their love, to the point where I had to be careful not to cry on the painting and smudge it! I would normally work with pastels and sometimes I would watch in amazement as they seemed to merge and flow on their own as I was guided to place the pastels upon the paper.

You can try the photograph technique for yourself. Play some soft music, turn off your phone and place the photograph of your pet on your lap. It's best if you can find a photo with a clear view of your pet's eyes. Send out a cord of love, visualizing it entering the heart of the animal in the photograph. Imagine that you can send all your love along that cord, and remember a happy time with your pet when you felt very connected to them—perhaps a favourite walk or ride, or giving them a treat that they enjoyed. Or sit in a favourite spot where your pet loved to lie. Then un-focus your eyes as though looking through the photo, asking the animal to show you what form it might return in, and see if you can intuit any images. You may be surprised to see a completely different species or breed of animal. Try not to dismiss your visions as just imagination or wishful thinking; just write them down and see what happens. Timelines can be a little hazy, as time in spirit is difficult to calibrate with time here on the physical plane, but be patient and see what comes your way.

You may also get images of your past-life connections with your pet. As we've seen in the past chapters, your pet could well have been a human—this may explain the incredible bond that you have shared in this lifetime, so don't be shocked or sceptical if you see this kind of vision. The secret is to be open; if you're coming from a place of love, you can't go far wrong. If you should get any negative images or feelings about a past trauma, be creative in imagining how it could be changed into a far happier outcome and choose this outcome instead. Our minds are incredibly powerful and we can achieve a great deal if we work with a positive intention. Be alert to connections and notice how information you are given about a past life may impact or mirror something that is happening in your current life. Always remember that by healing the past, we really can alter and improve our present situations.

Chakra Healing

As we've seen in previous chapters, working with the chakras can create wonderful healing and an instant emotional 'barometer' as to how we're feeling on deep levels. Of course our pets have similar physical chakra systems, which you can work with in the same way. Work through the seven major chakras of either you or your pet, inviting an image, colour, word or feeling as you focus on each one. If anything seems 'sludgy' or negative, just visualize pouring in white light, transmuting the image into something much more positive. It can be interesting to write your visualizations down every time you do this exercise; things may change, which is fine as long as you remain open and curious and alert to things that seem to be out of balance.

Working with imagery and symbolism in this way is fantastic for cutting through the anxieties of whether or not we will actually be able to 'see' and glean information. Our subconscious works very well with imagery and always gives us exactly what we need in order to heal ourselves and intuit the needs of our pets. Always finish this exercise by wrapping yourself and your pet in the light, visualizing perhaps a beautiful bubble of white light. If it works better for you, you can also visualize each chakra as a beautiful flower and decide how open you would like to be within each centre, by symbolically choosing the level of openness of each flower, from a tight bud to a full bloom. This will help you to protect and preserve your energy flow when interacting with the outside world, where taking on other people's emotions and feelings can be draining.

We obviously looked at the chakra system earlier in the book, but here is a quick reminder.

- BASE CHAKRA. Very base of the spine, connected with feelings of security and the colour red.
- SACRAL CHAKRA. Centre of the pelvis, connected to identity and validation and to sexuality. Normally associated with the colour orange.
- SOLAR PLEXUS CHAKRA. Just above the navel, associated with self-worth, digestive organs and the colour yellow.
- HEART CHAKRA. Centre of the chest, associated with self-love, heart and lungs and the colours pink and green.
- THROAT CHAKRA. Connected to the neck and mouth, self-expression and the colour sky blue.
- THIRD EYE CHAKRA. Centre of the forehead, the seat of our intuition. Connected with eyes and ears and the colour indigo.
- CROWN CHAKRA. Top of the head, associated with our personal power and connection with spirit. Normally associated with the colours violet or white.

Don't underestimate the power of the chakra-visualizing exercise for either you or your animals: it really can change energy at a very deep level and is extremely useful, the quicker you become at performing it, for immediately bringing your attention to areas that need balancing either physically or otherwise.

Animal Guides

Native Americans believe that each animal has its own 'medicine'. They define this as a strength or quality that the animal can share with us. So, just as we can have human spirit guides, we can also have special animals who have chosen to come through to us to help us. These may be animals that have shared lifetimes with us (like my beloved Pillow) or animals that we have never connected with before in a physical sense. Sometimes, quite unusual and unexpected animals can come through to guide us. To call in your animal guide, switch off all distractions like phones. Lighting a candle, if that is something you like, can help to set your intention and make this into a special occasion. Again if it feels right, play some soft music. Find yourself a comfortable chair where you can sit with your feet firmly placed on the floor, as crossing your legs can block energy flow. Place your hands on your knees with palms facing upwards and take some deep but gentle breaths, sending any chattery thoughts on their way. With each out-breath allow yourself to sink a little more into a relaxed state. Send out a request for your animal guide to come forward or make its presence felt, and be open to whatever comes into your mind—it may be an image, or a name, or just a feeling that something has drawn close. Thank them for stepping forward and being willing to help you. You may now wish to ask them if they can help you with your problems—listen quietly, see what comes to mind and trust your intuition. Remember that this is how we start to stretch the intuitive 'muscles' that we all possess. Write down any impressions you receive. When you feel that it's time to finish, always thank your guides for drawing close and for being of service.

You may continue to receive further information in your dreams, as sometimes the conscious mind and analytical processes interfere with us receiving and processing information on this level.

Conclusion

Each of us is a seed that was planted in our world's current vibration. When we raise our own frequencies through the growth produced by life challenges, we raise the world's frequency from within. Like a single drop of dye added to a glass of water, each person alters the entire hue. As we create feelings of joy, even if we do so while living alone on a mountain top, we emit a frequency that makes it easier for others to be joyful. As we create feelings of peace, we resonate an energy that helps to end wars. As we love we make it easier for others, both those whom we meet and those who will never know us, to love. Who we are therefore is far more meaningful than anything we may ever do.

ROBERT SCHWARTZ, *YOUR SOUL'S PLAN*

Knowing that we have an eternal connection can reassure and comfort us when having to cope with the pain of loss when our animals pass. Sadly, the difference in life spans between humans and most animals means that many animals will pass through our lives. The good news, though, is that they can come back whenever they want. The following are some stories of how my current animal family came to me. I wanted to end with some stories of my own animal family. I find them so inspiring and supportive in my work and they continually remind me of the issues that my clients and all of us face. These experiences have reaffirmed my belief in our deep connections and the sure knowledge I feel that death is also life—just in another dimension.

"Shame about those kittens!" I overheard someone saying as I stood in the long, slow queue in my village post office. "I suppose they'll have to be drowned if no one wants them. They're a bit wild—don't know what happened to their mother," continued the speaker at the head of the queue. Craning to see who was talking, I saw that it was a man, a pensioner, conversing with a woman of a similar age. Forsaking my place in the queue,

I approached the man and asked him for more information about the kittens. He told me they'd been abandoned in a garden under a shrub, and as it was the middle of winter he was amazed they'd survived this long. I asked if I might be able to go and look at them, as I would be willing to give a home to one and might also be able to find homes for the others if they needed them. The man took me to see the kittens and, searching under the bushes, I spied a flash of silver stripes. This bundle of fluff stood its ground defiantly, hissing and puffing itself up. It had the most beautiful markings and extraordinarily large eyes. It was love at first sight. I quickly ran home to find a box to collect it, along with its tabby siblings, but by the time I got back to the garden someone else had taken them. At least, I thought all of the kittens had gone, but suddenly I saw the silver kitten peeking out from a bush at the far end of the garden. After much calling and making soothing sounds, the stripy kitten finally stepped forward tentatively, creeping ever closer to me, and eventually let me pick it up. I tucked it inside my coat out of the cold and carried it home.

Zappa

Had I known at the time what was to become of this dear little cat, I might not have been so keen to offer him a home, but I realize now that everything that unfolds in our lives, good and bad, is all pre-agreed and co-created. I marvel at the way the Universe orchestrates the reunion of souls and also how committed our animal friends are to finding us again to continue our mutual soul journeys.

At home, the kitten, who I named Zappa, settled in well and became very affectionate. I had planned to have him neutered when he was old enough, but my partner at the time persuaded me to leave him 'entire', or uncastrated, and stupidly I now think, I agreed. Unfortunately, this meant that Zappa was forever marking his territory around the village and going into our neighbours' homes, stealing their own cats' food and spraying his scent, much to their annoyance. I finally decided to take him to the vet for neutering without telling my partner, but before I could do it my partner took things into his own hands and shot my lovely cat. Perhaps needless to say, our partnership ended pretty quickly after that! I was horribly upset — this beautiful cat had become so affectionate and trusting and this was how we humans had repaid him. I mourned his loss and the dreadful way in which he had lost his life.

Years later, when my eldest son was little and at primary school, his best friend told him that his mother's cat had had kittens. My son came home from school asking if we might have one, and I agreed to take him to look at the litter. There was a lovely silver tabby kitten, but we were told that it had already been reserved. Something about one of the other tabby kittens seemed to call to me, however; he seemed very confident and busily clambered up my lap and stared into my eyes. There was something about his eyes that stirred a deep memory and I knew that this was the one for us. We named him Zappa after his beautiful predecessor. When we brought him home he marched into the house, gave a huge spit and hiss at our aged collie, did a pee in his litter tray and settled down as if he owned the place. He was never a cuddly cat — he was affectionate only when he chose to be, and always appeared to have an 'attitude'. He would purr if strangers were foolhardy enough to stroke him, even though we would warn them, and then without warning launch his attack — usually resulting in bloodshed. With the children, as long as they showed him respect he never drew blood, but he would admonish them if he felt they had crossed some invisible line in the way they handled him. We loved him for his character and strength. We also made sure we had him neutered at the appropriate age, but I was to find out that this didn't really help his opinion of humans much. After several years of him believing that we lived with him rather than the reverse, I asked him with my newfound telepathic skills why he had always been a bit of a grouch. His reply was succinct and straight to the point, to say the least: "Well, you cut my balls off — what do you expect!!" I tried to explain that I had just been trying to prevent a repeat of the problems we'd had with his predecessor, but getting my point of view across to this feisty, quirky cat proved rather difficult.

These little problems aside, we loved and respected this cat for almost seventeen years. He was absolutely a part of the fabric of our home. One weekend, though, we noticed that he was starting to stumble. During the following day he deteriorated and the left side of his face took on an appearance as if it had fallen in. His balance was also affected and he kept falling over, while his left eye made alarming flicking movements. I rushed him to the vet, where they agreed that he'd probably had a stroke and gave him some medication. Sadly though, he never improved and so we made the only decision we could. When we brought his body home to be buried, he seemed to have a peaceful smiley expression on his face. I told him he should come back to us if he felt able, and thanked him for being the most wonderful cat and for sharing his life with us. In life he had had the most expressive whiskers—they would fan out like a walrus when the prospect of a tasty food morsel was headed his way. His whiskers took on that look as I spoke to him in his box, and I stroked them, trying to imprint the memory of his lovely face in my heart forever.

Zappa was buried in his favourite sunny spot in our garden, with a terracotta plaque my daughter brought back from Italy that reads, in honour of his feisty nature, ATTENTI IL GATTO or 'Beware of the cat!'

Giza

After seventeen years of Zappa's presence in our lives, his absence left a huge void. Even the dogs, who had been ruled by his paw of iron, seemed to miss him. After a couple of months I mentioned our sad loss to my lovely homoeopathic vet friend Judith, who smiled and suggested that I look in the box in the corner of her kitchen.

There was a newly born litter of kittens! Their mother was a fluffy silver tabby with a beautiful temperament and their father was a stray, or feral, tabby. I remembered that Zappa's father had also been feral. Judith told me I could have the pick of the litter when they were old enough. Although they were all beautiful, one kitten, a male, was a mix of silver and traditional tabby colouring and also sported wonderful stripes and spots. Every time I went to see Judith, and saw him again, he seemed to stand out from all the other kittens.

When I arrived to take him home, Judith greeted me with the words: "I hope you're ready for this—yours is a thug!" I stepped into the kitchen to see my kitten swinging from the ear of an ancient, extremely patient springer spaniel. I felt strongly that this was Zappa coming back to me—certainly this 'new Zappa' seemed to have all the confidence and disdain of the last one. There was another kitten left unclaimed, and when I saw my kitten cuddled up companionably with this last one it seemed so unfair to leave him behind, so I took them both home. Back at the house the new Zappa behaved exactly as the last one had—he spat at the dogs, who seemed to instantly recognize him and the new shift in the balance of power.

Anneka

The other kitten just looked up at me, and I got a very strange feeling followed by a message in my head telling me that he was Anneka, my lovely goat from years ago, who had told me from spirit she would return as a cat. Anneka had also told me that she would be a male cat and that I should call him Thebes, after the ancient Egyptian city state. She said that she had wanted to experience being an indoor animal and to be able to snuggle up in my bed — something, to be honest, that she would have done as a goat if she'd been allowed! We decided to call our new Zappa Giza, after another area of Egypt. We liked the fact that this name, with its Z and A, had a similarity to Zappa and therefore a continuity. My son also liked the fact that the name sounded like 'Geezer' — very appropriate, as he certainly seemed to be living up to the name!

Giza is becoming more and more like his previous incarnation, but he is far more loving and less fierce this time round, which makes me think and hope that all his past trauma has been healed and that we can have many happy years together without too many wounds. Thebes is like a limpet, glued to my chest at every opportunity, like Anneka in the past; we have the most amazing connection.

Giza and Thebes

He has what I would describe as a leonine countenance, and one day I finally made the connection between this and Anneka — she had had very intense yellow eyes, and I suddenly realized that of course she must have been a lion in a past incarnation.

We had probably been lions together. I'm often quite overwhelmed when I think about the amount of love with which our animals continue to maintain our connections. The two cats have also started to help me with my healing sessions with human clients, including recently helping someone with a very traumatic past-life issue.

Fascinatingly, during this session Thebes was sitting next to the client giving support. However, she said she could feel his paw on her foot, grounding her. When she looked at it though, it looked not like the dainty paw of a domestic cat but like a huge lion paw!

Thebes working in my healing room

Very sadly, during the writing process on this book, my beautiful Thebes was tragically killed on the road. In agonizing times like this it's very hard to fathom the reasons as to why such things happen, especially when Thebes was still so young. It can seem such a waste of a life.

It's the physical contact we miss and crave so much when any loved one passes, and it is the same for me with Thebes. He has 'told' me from spirit that, like my dog Pillow, he found being in his physical form too challenging, as he was sensitive to so much of the world's pain. Although externally he was a rough-and-tumble mouser, I always felt that there was a part of him that was too gentle for this world. He says that in spirit he can expand his energy field and give much more healing and guidance to this troubled world. He proved he was a master healer in his life with me when he was only two months old. Although his passing is hard to bear, I feel him all around me, and I look forward to the wisdom I know he will share with me and to our future reconnections. I adored Anneka, his previous incarnation, but she also had a fragility about her. Sometimes we feel that we cannot or must not open our hearts again to the risk of more pain, but what blessings we are given by the love of our animals! I would not have missed out on that for anything. I hope that when I see cases of similar tragedies with my clients, Thebes will guide me as to the best way to comfort them. He gave me so much love as he purred and kneaded his way into my heart, to remain there forever.

Cats leave paw prints on our hearts
ANONYMOUS

When my lovely dog Pillow died, I felt she had left the earthly plane so that our rescue dog Winnie could come into our lives. Winnie has proved to be the most wonderful dog and I feel she is a reincarnation of my gorgeous dog Auntie Weazle". I tell the following story to illustrate just how awesome Winnie is.

> One day, my son was sitting at the table doing his homework and Winnie was sitting under his chair, which was a little unusual. Suddenly, she started to shake violently, which was very worrying as I'd never seen her do it before. I asked her telepathically what was wrong and she 'told' me that there was something my son wasn't telling me and that she was worried about him. I questioned him and, like a typical teenager, he was non-committal and just mumbled that everything was OK. I encouraged him to speak up, saying that we really couldn't have Winnie worrying and shaking like this, and he finally opened up and told me that he was struggling with his A-level subjects and was getting increasingly worried about his exams. Winnie immediately started to wag her tail and looked much happier.

We have arranged for extra tuition for my son, and things are now much better for him. Winnie always tells me if he's had a difficult day or has any problems. She even told me once that he couldn't go out because he hadn't brushed his teeth, and when questioned he admitted that he hadn't, and was none too pleased about his canine friend 'grassing him up'! However, he loves that Winnie cares about him so much. She also helps me when I run animal communication courses and gives everybody 'readings', even sometimes bringing in their loved ones from spirit.

Most Saturdays at around 5.55pm she will sit in the window seat in the lounge that looks out onto the driveway, waiting for my son's father to bring my son back. She always knows when the time—6pm—is getting close, and will take up her position and await his arrival. Winnie is the epitome of gentleness and caring concern, and again I can only marvel at the animals' commitment to continuing to love and care for us. All this brings me to the incredible revelation that my little terrier, Teazle, has returned after a much longer lapse of time.

Auntie Weazle

My border terrier Teazle had insisted on joining me in a craniosacral treatment from my friend Anna. The dog seemed to be trying to sit on my head, which was a little distracting, so I offered to put her outside the room. Anna surprised me by saying no, Teazle had to be there. I had always found it quite difficult to communicate with Teazle, as we are very close emotionally and I know that she takes on physical and emotional issues for me. This distresses me, as obviously I don't like her suffering because of me, but I have to remember that our pets will sometimes take on our physical ailments as part of their incredible commitment to us.

Teazle

*"Unconditional love leaves you
hairy and smelling of dog".*

TEAZLE

However I wasn't prepared for Anna's revelation as to exactly why Teazle and I were so close. As Anna worked, she told me that she'd begun to get some very strange images in her head. She said that Teazle was showing her our soul connection from light years ago and from different planets. It made me very emotional, and amazed that she had chosen to come back to me after all this time. I had always called her my 'teddy', as she wanted to be cuddled into my lap at every available opportunity and constantly shadows me—even into the loo! What better way to show me her unconditional love than by returning as a cuddly canine. She had been a birthday present from my husband and has proved to be the best present I could ever have wished for.

Madeleine with Teazle and Winnie

The following account is of yet another animal working hard to find its way back to me in the most surprising, quite relentless way!

> I'd been called to a farm on Dartmoor to visit a pony with behavioural problems. When I'd finished, I happened to glance into another stable and there, huddled at the back, defiantly looking back at me, was a young horse with the most incredible markings I had ever seen. I asked the owner about him and she told me that she'd just bought him from a farm in Cornwall because she'd felt sorry for him. He was in poor condition and seemed to have a very dim view of the human race. I said that he looked like a Jackson Pollock painting, with his striking 'spattered' markings. From then on, the frightened little horse haunted my thoughts; I couldn't stop thinking about him. Night and day his image would come into my head and one day I was compelled to ring his owner, who was a horse dealer, and ask that, as odd as it may seem at the time, that if she should ever sell him, could she give my details to the new owners to give me first refusal. I was in no position to buy him then, as I was about to move house and didn't have the funds or time to home a horse. To my surprise his owner said that she would love me to have him. I explained my situation, but she said that she'd keep him for me as she was in no hurry to sell him.

My house sale fell through, leaving me feeling unable to contemplate having a horse in my life again. I decided to ring the dealer and tell her that I felt that this horse had to be in a new 'forever' home and that it wasn't fair to keep them both waiting on some vague future hope that my position might change. However, the Universe had other ideas — as soon as I rang her, words tumbled out of my mouth completely beyond my control, and I put the phone down having agreed to a buying price and to pay for his keep until I could collect him. To this day I don't know how that happened. I remember laughing to myself as I wondered where the words had come from. Of course, the little horse was orchestrating things perfectly. I found someone to take him on for me until my position on the housing front became clearer. I asked if he might be gently schooled into being a ridden horse through natural horsemanship, as traditional methods had not worked with him due to bad handling in a previous home. Unfortunately, he was resistant to this approach as well. So I mentioned him to a shaman friend of mine, who then told me that the reason this was happening was that the horse was a reincarnation of my medicine horse from a previous lifetime when I had been a Northern Cree medicine woman. My friend said that the horse had to be called by his native name or he would continue his bad behaviour. When I asked my Shaman friend how on earth to achieve this, he just told me that it would come to me.

One day soon after, some strange words popped into my head — Wah Chee Hah: Thunder Horse. I immediately texted my shaman friend, who agreed that these were indeed Native American words, and so the horse was named. As things were still not going to plan financially, I asked a client one day if she might be interested in a little spotty horse. She surprised me by replying, "What, Wah Chee?"

I don't know to this day why I mentioned it, as all of her other horses were very smart dressage types and she had previously told me that she disliked 'coloured' horses like this one. But Wah Chee obviously had everything in hand, as she explained that ever since she had heard me talk about him and seen him on my website, she couldn't stop thinking about him. In fact, she admitted sheepishly that she had felt 'forced' by some unknown power to look at his picture on my website at least once a day. I was thrilled — I knew that she would give him the most wonderful home of the kind that I was at that time unable to give him. He now resides in luxury with a lovely retired chestnut mare for a friend; his only duties are that his owner and I consult him for help with our problems.

Wah Chee

There are many diverse beings coexisting on this planet and I believe we are all part of the 'one', a collective consciousness. I believe that we go through many incarnations, not only as other planetary beings but in many different guises and at different vibrations, in order to grow at a soul level. I believe we need to experience differing levels of vibrational bodies to evolve and anchor our true light bodies — in some lifetimes we are very enlightened beings while in others we are at a decidedly lower vibration, with no spiritual aspirations, and that is fine; it is all part of our journey.

I also feel that soul beings in animal form are experiencing those vibrations in order to learn and experience different facets of being. In many ways, animals seem more highly evolved in their awareness because they have not suppressed or limited their instinctive or intuitive 'antennae', as we humans have been conditioned to do. Ancient tribal cultures communicated with every aspect of nature, believing that everything had a soul or its own special energy. They also communicated telepathically over vast distances; the concept of telepathy was the norm. Sadly, it no longer is.

In regressive states, people are enabled to reconnect with the past-life incarnations of present-day partners, people and animals, and with situations with which they have difficult issues. Once people discover these connections, healing can take place and challenges can be resolved.

Many religions believe that species are interchangeable and that we are all inextricably connected. If this is true, it makes sense that any animal can be aware of a great deal that happens in its environment. It follows that they have a deep understanding of the emotional and physical issues that their human companions are experiencing. If we open to the possibility and 'remember' our former skills, it needn't be so surprising or challenging that we can all communicate. However, in our western cultures we are encouraged to focus on materialistic, left-brain notions and lifestyles. In this way we, often unknowingly, 'blinker' ourselves and restrict our intuitive powers.

As humans and animals, then, we are all on our respective journeys of enlightenment, and we must all make sure that we learn from and enjoy the blessings these journeys bring. I am continually humbled by my own animals and by all the beautiful creatures I have been fortunate enough to work with. I feel blessed to have been called to work with them in this way. I thank all my animal teachers for their patience and love along the way; I am eternally indebted to them for showering me with their wisdom. I pray that you too feel wrapped in wisdom and love from our eternal soul animal friends.

Acknowledgements

Huge thanks to Findhorn Press for their continued support in publishing my work. I am so grateful to them for helping me get the animals' voices and messages heard. Big thanks to Sabine, Thierry, Carol, Gail and Jacqui for their help. Also to Jenny Smedley, who was kind enough to write the foreword and who has been a driving force behind my writing, a huge thank you. I thank Thea Holly for her wisdom and for sharing her healing techniques; they have helped me and my clients so much. Thanks to Robert Schwartz for allowing me to refer to his illuminating book. I would also like to thank all my clients and friends who have agreed to allow me to tell their stories as part of the book, illustrating how incredible the animals are. Some names have been changed for privacy. Big thanks to Flick Cromak, Victoria Standen, Pam Lovett, Leigh Jackson, Sera Henbest, Sylvia Davalos, Fiona Habershon and Cynthia Starkey for granting permission to use their photos.

I would also like to send my love to all my animals, past and present, for all their continued support and guidance, reassuring me that we are all destined to journey together again and again and that nothing is ever 'lost' at all (thank you Pillow!) It has been something of a vertical learning curve since the lovely Jack Russell Sam opened my mind to the concepts of interspecies communication and shared past lives with our animals. I hope I have done my animal teachers justice in my continued commitment to helping raise awareness of how much we need to learn from the animals. I wonder where my life would have led without that fateful day, sitting in a farmhouse kitchen cuddling a tiny puppy who changed my life forever!

Treasured Friend

I lost a treasured friend today
The little dog who used to lay
Her gentle head upon my knee
And share her silent thoughts with me…
She'll come no longer to my call
Retrieve no more her favourite ball
A voice far greater than my own
Has called her to His golden throne.
Although my eyes are filled with tears,
I thank Him for the happy years
He let her spend down here with me
And for her love and loyalty.
When it is time for me to go
And join her there, this much I know…
I shall not fear the transient dark
For she will greet me with her bark.

AUTHOR UNKNOWN

Resources

Madeleine Walker
www.anexchangeoflove.com

Scentsations Protector Drops
scentsations@shaw.ca

Grue Demoiselle Retreat, Limoges, Limousin, France
www.gruedemoiselle.com

House of Swallows Retreat, Moncarapacho, Eastern Algarve, Portugal
http://www.spiritualretreatalgarve.com

Gateway 2 ranch retreat, Liz Mitten Ryan
www.equinisity.com

International Flower Essence Repertoire
www.ifer.co.uk

Beautiful healing essences
www.healingorchids.com

Judith Webster, Homoeopathic Veterinary Surgeon
44 (0) 1822 820251 (UK)
judith@nat-vet.co.uk

Anna Atkinson, Craniosacral Therapy
44 (0)1209 890538 (UK)

Hoofbeats Equine Rehabilitation Sanctuary, Shaugh Prior, Plymouth UK
www.hoofbeats.org.uk

Bibliography

De Dan, Rose. *Tails of a Healer*, Milton Keynes, UK: Authorhouse, 2008.

Glouberman, Dina. *Life Choices, Life Changes*, San Rafael, CA: Mandala, 1989.

Lipton, Bruce. *The Biology of Belief*, London: Hay House, 2008.

Lipton, Bruce. *Spontaneous Evolution*, London: Hay House, 2009.

Mitten Ryan, Liz. *The Truth According to Horses*, Kamloops, BC Canada: Booksurge Publishing, 2008.

Smedley, Jenny. *Pets Have Souls Too*, London: Hay House, 2009.

Schwartz, Robert. *Your Soul's Plan*, Berkeley, CA: Frog Books/North Atlantic Books, 2009.

Walker, Madeleine. *An Exchange of Love*, Ropley, Hants, UK: O Books, 2008.

Walker, Madeleine. *The Whale Whisperer*, Forres, Scotland: Findhorn Press, 2011.

Other books by Madeleine Walker

*An Exchange of Love: Animals Healing People
in Past, Present, and Future Lifetimes*

*The Whale Whisperer: Healing Messages from the
Animal Kingdom to Help Mankind and the Planet*

Whale Whispers, Lion Roars
(channelled meditation CD)

Fearless Earth
(channelled meditation CD),
with Jerome O'Connell

FINDHORN PRESS

Life-Changing Books

For a complete catalogue,
please contact:

Findhorn Press Ltd
117-121 High Street,
Forres IV36 1AB,
Scotland, UK

t +44 (0)1309 690582
f +44 (0)131 777 2711
e info@findhornpress.com

or consult our catalogue online
(with secure order facility) on
www.findhornpress.com

For information on the Findhorn Foundation:
www.findhorn.org